yearning for love

yearning for love

A RELUCTANT DIVORCEE'S ROCKY ROAD TO NIRVANA

Katherine Barton

ÉRIU HOUSE
St. Paul, MN

Yearning for Love: A Reluctant Divorcee's Rocky Road to Nirvana
Published by Ériu House, St. Paul, MN

Print ISBN 979-8-218-49398-1
E-book ISBN 979-8-218-49399-8

Cover photo: *Merry Maidens, Ancient Site near Penzance, Cornwall, at the Break of Day* by Roger Driscoll, iStock by Getty Images

Cover design by Jeenee Lee
Page design by Beth Wright, Wright for Writers LLC

To learn more about Katherine Barton

visit **kabarton.com**

Nothing that is worth doing can be achieved in our lifetime; therefore we must be saved by hope. Nothing which is true or beautiful makes complete sense in any immediate context of history; therefore we must be saved by faith. Nothing we do, however virtuous, can be accomplished alone; therefore, we are saved by love.

—Reinhold Niebuhr, *The Irony of American History*

The mysterious path of life comes with no manual. I am sadly aware that if there was one, I would refuse to follow it when I needed it most.

—Anonymous

Saying love has to come from a strong place, not just grabbing whatever's in reach.

—Barbara Kingsolver, *Demon Copperhead*

Prologue

The mossy rocks stand about four feet tall in a circle, their corners rounded like a worn piece of soap. Some lean back a little while others sit comfortably in the soil.

I think of the Merry Maidens, the story that accompanies this ancient circle. One night nineteen maidens were caught dancing on Sunday by the local police, otherwise known as priests. The covey of enforcers cursed the maidens into eternity, transforming them into stones that stand today, thousands of years later, for all to see.

I have traveled to this place outside Penzance, England, to perform a ritual of beginning. In the last four years, my marriage ended, and my only child went off to college half a continent away; I had moved out of my dream house, retired, contracted a chronic illness, and witnessed the death of my beloved stepmother.

I needed and deserved—I thought—a new beginning with the same urgency a choking victim needs the Heimlich maneuver.

I approach the stones with a package of tobacco in my hand, an indigenous symbol of prayer and respect. I sprinkle a pinch on each rock in gratitude for the past, along with fervent prayers for a happier and more peaceful future. I optimistically hope that the trials of recent years are over and a twenty-first-century version of nirvana will make a speedy appearance. The gesture is keenly satisfying, marking my aspirations for a new life and extending a hearty welcome to a long absent sense of vitality.

My mission complete, I turn away and enter a taxi. Before the driver starts the engine, he convinces me to take a side trip to a nearby *quoit*, or giant's table in the Cornish language. I consent and end up spending another fifty pounds viewing the oversized relic that adds little to the trip other than income to my cagey chauffeur.

For four years, I was on a journey I hadn't planned. I found myself feeling as paralyzed and cursed as the stony maidens while being equally susceptible to unnecessary and expensive side trips. At that time, I didn't know that the years of confusion, grief, and denial were not over. I was ending one cycle, but the next one would have its own formidable demons to tame.

As the taxi drives away, I look down at my hand and see shreds of tobacco still sticking to my palm. I brush them off and sigh as I board a train, blissfully unaware of what is to come.

PART I

Chapter 1

I awoke on a Saturday morning and knew with utmost certainty that my marriage was over. I had no doubts, no maybes, no wiggle room, no "Let's try this!" or "but ifs." We had tried everything. Nothing remained but a sense of embittered defeat.

It was May 2013, a few months short of our twentieth anniversary. For decades, I had avoided this tormenting knowledge while maintaining a covey of therapists, energy workers, psychics, and marriage counselors with credentials ranging from impeccable to sketchy. Although my spouse refused to consult with anyone with crystals in their office, we saw one marriage counselor for more than twelve years in the elusive hope that his presence could reinvigorate our union. Meanwhile, our marriage became a dirge that I chose not to hear.

The dozens of marriage books I had devoured with hope mocked me on my bedstand. The titles guaranteed to save my partnership included everything from John Gottman's *The Seven Principles for Making Marriage Work* to Elizabeth Gilbert's *Committed.*

On the morning of my epiphany, salty water rolled down my cheek, hitting the blue-and-maroon sheets John had bought while I was out of town years before. They were the ugliest sheets I had seen before or since. What a bizarre accident that these decorative infractions were the first witnesses to my unwilling acceptance.

I had ignored the most recent omens. Twice that week I walked down the asphalt path to the Mississippi River I had trod for twenty-seven years. On the first occasion, I had stood at my familiar overlook and had a strange sensation that I was on fire. It was as if someone had thrown kerosene on a forgotten nook of my soul, sparking a tower of invisible flames.

Two days later, I stopped cold on the pathway overlooking the watery valley as I heard a voice in my head that said, "Lose the weight."

That same week I had a dream. I was in a fenced pen outside a farmhouse. A snake appeared and tried to squeeze into the hose used for watering livestock. Someone came out the front door and shouted, "Don't let it in! If you do, the snake will take over the whole house."

Dismissing my nocturnal vision, I continued my day, willfully thinking that nothing was amiss as we attended a financial review of our retirement funds. The friendly advisor greeted us with a big smile, his hands folded on our report, "You are in great shape for the long run! Nothing to worry about at all!"

I looked at John sitting next to me at the laminated plastic table in the windowless conference room. I recalled our conversation about hiring this advisor.

"We need to hire a planner," I had said, repeating a frequent request.

He sighed. "I've been taking care of this for years. Those clowns never tell me anything I don't know."

I tried to be calm. I desperately wanted an outside opinion. My father's foreboding message, "Money! It don't come back!" was a constant internal companion along with his diatribe about supporting his family on three dollars a week during the Depression. Income was a commodity that could disappear at any moment, leaving me helpless and adrift. Although we had infrequent briefings with Excel spreadsheets, they consistently left me feeling confused and doubtful about our future. If I heard it from someone "official," I could attain a much-desired sense of safety about my material future. Tired of my badgering, John finally relented, and here we were.

My husband had no visible reaction to the advisor's celebratory pronouncement. I knew his stoicism hid his disdain for both the advisor's expertise and his profession. I had never acknowledged that our positive financial situation was largely due to John's dedication to tracking our investments as he sat holed up in his office for days at a time. Worse, I had criticized him for not saving more and doubted him when he assured me that things were fine. At that moment in the sterile room, I wanted to pull him closer in gratitude. I noticed I hadn't felt such an urge for a long time.

As we walked to the car, I was buoyant. "That was great, didn't you think! I'm really happy."

He looked at me squarely. "I told you," he said sullenly. "Nothing new there."

That evening, we were planning to attend a high-end gala staffed by a dear friend. I had taken the unusual step of buying a new dress, a perk I customarily avoided. It was hard to find something I liked that fit my expanding waistline and smoothed out the bumps in my hips. But this time I had succeeded and felt shyly attractive and upbeat as I stood tall in a puffy, voile pink top with a black chiffon skirt. Standing next to my husband in his appealing dark suit, I bashfully assumed we formed an attractive couple.

When we arrived, John turned to me in the parking lot and spoke in a tone he used when chastising me for not loading the dishwasher properly.

"Look at your shoes. What's wrong with them?" He pointed to a tiny hole on the side of my left pump I had camouflaged with tape that almost matched. His comment was as painful as a wasp's stinger jabbing into my forearm. Later, after we settled at our table, he became enmeshed in conversation about solar power with a fellow wearing a bow tie and horn-rimmed glasses. I pulled him up to dance with me as he continued to chatter about the latest discovery in energy technology. I moved his drooping hand above my waist in an attempt to engage his attention as he looked around the room.

To comfort myself, I conjured up a familiar image that soothed me. The picture was an isolated woman with windswept, raven hair that hung like forsaken strings from a tired mop. Trudging across an arid and tree-less plain, the thin body clutched a heavy, olive-green cloak around her shoulders to block out the piercing wind in a feeble attempt at warmth. Her brown sandals, once elegant, were now in disrepair, the straps scuffed and the tarnished buckles hanging askew. She had become an expert at grasping the woolen garment tightly against her body as the gusty wind arose, even though it was becoming an increasing burden for her as the cool weather changed to a sweltering heat. Her fingernails were blue, less from the frigid air than from clenching the garment with her diminished strength. She believed if she could just hold the cloak tightly enough, she would be safe and secure.

I had clung to this figure for years, grasping it like a favorite stuffed tiger providing solace to a toddler. It didn't matter that the toy was missing an ear and its tail hung like a discarded rag. On the dance floor that evening, the cloaked figure disappeared from my imagination, and I was left with my reluctant dance partner, deeply disappointed in what I thought would be a magical evening.

A few weeks before, I wanted a mirror installed on the back of our bedroom door. John brought one home, a plain, big-box variety with a narrow black plastic frame. It needed two sets of hands to mount it.

He stood on the bare oak floor in our bedroom doorway wearing a faded yellow button-down shirt and washed-out jeans he had bought at a thrift store. He leaned over into his three-tiered toolbox and pulled out an electric screwdriver and four screws.

"Hold these," he said, handing me the screws. I held out my hand, my upper arms swaying like little hammocks in my loose blue sweatshirt with white letters saying "Orthodox Druid." To avoid stepping on yesterday's underwear, I stepped back and moved my head to get a sense of the right angle. He held the mirror up so I could check the placement.

"Right here?" he asked, holding it off-center.

"No, a little this way," I said, as I gestured to the left.

He moved it down, so my head was cut off.

"Higher," I said.

"You're taking it the other way," he said impatiently.

I ignored him, pulling it out of his hand and adjusting it myself, nodding in agreement.

"This works," I said.

Sighing he said, "Take this side while I anchor it."

I wrapped my hands around the left side, intending to let his machine pierce the door with a loud hum. Instead, my hand slipped, and the mirror headed downward. We both grabbed it, rescuing it a few inches from the floor, preventing a mosaic of shattered glass on the polished surface.

He looked at me accusingly. "I said hold onto it!"

"I did," I said loudly. "I thought you would move the other way!"

He closed his eyes and breathed heavily. In a highly controlled voice he said, "Here. Hold it while I screw it in." I silently obeyed him, and this time it held. He added two extra screws to avoid future problems. Curling his lip, he placed the screwdriver back into the toolbox.

Defiant, I headed downstairs to make dinner. My hand automatically grabbed a handful of cashews out of a jar on the counter and tossed them into my mouth as I waited for the chicken to finish.

He came downstairs wearing a secondhand fleece vest.

"I'm going to a volleyball game," he said.

"I thought we could have a family dinner together," I said.

"Game's at six," he said, reaching for a stick of celery. "I'll grab something there."

I looked down into the pan. I wasn't hungry. It was only a little tiff, that's all, I thought. My mind insisted there was nothing wrong and there was no crisis. My hand just went the wrong way, and the mirror was now satisfactorily hung. Yet the assurance and comfort of a family dinner was not to happen this evening despite my preparation.

I told myself I didn't need to hold onto this brief power struggle over such a minor incident. I did sense, however, in those months leading up to that May morning, that the weather of my life was changing. A new season was in the air that would require an entirely different kind of protection, something far stronger than the woolen cloak worn by my imaginary companion.

In the past, other images ruled who I was. There was the annual holiday portrait where I stood with smiling family members, the youngest holding a cat. The Christmas tree held ornaments crafted years before by my daughter. I referred to my home, family, and marriage as wholeness, a fact that would cause bitter chuckles in future years. I believed we were domestic perfection and that marriage meant lifelong stability and happiness despite the well-known reality that half of married couples relinquish their vows. Their partnerships ended, I thought, because people weren't committed to one another and were fundamentally weak. Such an action was an unthinkable possibility in connection with myself, and though I wouldn't have uttered the word—a sin.

Cowering under the covers on that May morning, I saw myself reflected in the contentious mirror. A vicious sorrow welled up in my heart along with its terrifying relative: fear. I remembered the thousands of warnings I had ignored and the myths I had clung to. My elaborate subterfuge had finally run its course and I was face-to-face with the price of decades of denial.

This is what I get for trying to improve myself, I thought bitterly, penning the first chapter of my tome of unadulterated self-pity. I sorrowfully admitted that I would really rather have been an overweight, contented bimbo. My primary pastime could be eating maraschino cherries while watching Netflix with my tummy hanging out of sweatpants, happy with a partnership that had the emotional depth of Dan Quayle.

After lying awake for hours, I left my sleeping husband, got dressed, and met with a smiling, efficient mother from my daughter's school. She gave me detailed instructions on how to run the upcoming silent auction as I sat nodding, with a plastered-on smile as my stomach burned with acid.

Chapter 2

A teacher once declared to me that life is always thick with possibility. However, he cautioned, it is the past that truly determines the future. As I reflected on my now collapsed marriage, I had to agree with him and admit that the roots of its demise were both old and deep.

When I was four years old, I saw the legendary evangelist Billy Graham at Madison Square Garden in New York City. My sister and I held my mother's silky hands, clutching her long fingers to avoid being swallowed up by the overwhelming throng of followers on the barricaded Seventh Avenue. We held onto her tightly, careful not to scuff our patent leather shoes that set off our blue Sunday dresses. My mother wore her soft gray wool dress with fluffy snowballs, which she donned only for special occasions. My father stood on a car bumper so he could find us, wildly waving to get our attention in his wide-lapeled gray suit and narrow blue tie. Without honking taxis and impatient motorists, a fresh, meandering breeze surrounded the excited crowd, affirming that my family and I were in exactly the right place.

During the summers, I became a regular participant in "camp meetings" inside white, circus-sized tents in Northwest Georgia. The earth was covered with straw as white ladies waved crinkly paper fans embossed with the name Durgans, the local funeral home. The preacher's resonant, foreboding voice shouted from the makeshift pulpit as his outstretched arm held up a Bible.

"Come forward to the altar and kneel! *Give* your life to Jesus! Accepting Christ is the only way to get you to heaven and save you from the flames of hell!"

I always wanted to go up the center aisle to the altar when he voiced that passionate invitation. There was great appeal to being a member of this elite, chosen group of the faithful, despite the fact that the call was couched in a threat. Most of all, I yearned to be part of something undeniability right and good, with the blessing of an admiring community. But I hated the idea of a group of adults singling me out as the center of attention as they welcomed me to the flock. I preferred avoiding having my cheeks pinched by approving people twice my size. I therefore stayed in my seat, listening with fear and eagerness.

Back home at my church in suburban New Jersey, I gazed at portraits of John Wesley, the founder of Methodism. Every week, I stood in my short white socks, Mary Jane shoes and polka-dot dress with my ankles awkwardly crossed. I tilted my head as I looked at the artwork, hoping the other churchgoers would think I was thoughtfully examining the pictures for the first time. I wanted people to think I was merely interested, and not a girl without a pal to chat with.

I genuinely admired Wesley, a fiery and compassionate misfit. One etching showed him surrounded by a yellow glow, when he felt his "heart was strangely warmed." This contemplative feeling, so the story went, was the spark that created the Methodist Church, beginning with a scrappy, bold bunch of outcasts from the Church of England. Their obsession with sin was paired with a deep sense of contemplation and connection to divinity. Both qualities made a profound impression on me. I came to experience God as an agent of potential damnation but also as a positive, benevolent energy and cosmic cloud of comfort. As I got older, I sensed a powerful aura of goodness that became my basis for faith.

My early fascination wore off as I faced mandatory church attendance with a pastor who recited monotone eight-minute prayers with his eyes closed. At age ten, I feigned innocence and told my father that I didn't know what church meant so I should be excused from services.

That was the wrong tactic. He made me sit next to him during the entire service in the hard wooden pew as the giant painting of *The Last Supper* gazed down upon us. He scribbled multiple Bible verse messages in his illegible handwriting in the bulletin margin as he sat in his signature gray suit and tie.

I cringed. I had only asked because I wanted out, not because I wanted an explanation.

Later, my resistance grew bolder. One Sunday morning when I was fifteen, I refused to get out of bed to go to church. My older sister, Linda, crawled in beside me and attempted to push me onto the floor as I wrapped my arms around the mattress. My younger sister, Molly, pulled my legs from the side. Their efforts ended in a burst of giggles and bruises as we all crashed to the floor. Our fun complete, I was solemnly told to get dressed so we wouldn't be late.

It wasn't only the boring church service that I dreaded. My Sunday schoolteacher, Mr. Benjamin, had a voice with the inflection of a cow in need of milking. With peppery hair, he sat in his gray suit and bow tie, teaching us about the book of Daniel. He explained how, miraculously, Shadrach, Meshach, and Abednego were thrown into the fiery furnace and emerged unscathed. My grandmother particularly liked this story. As she told it, her eyes widened with excitement, in a lively testimony of how their faith allowed them to escape certain death "without burning a hair on their heads!"

In Mr. Benjamin's class, I prepared to bolt as the clock struck 9:30 a.m. Undeterred, he pulled out his pocket watch.

"One minute left!" he proclaimed.

Frustrated, I impatiently counted to sixty silently and bolted to liberation when the time was up.

The next year his high school–aged daughter became pregnant and, in midsixties jargon, "*had* to get married." My parents' discussion on the topic centered around the daughter's wrongful behavior and her father's disappointment in her. There was no mention of the impact on her: an adolescent having to abandon her own dreams to raise an unplanned child.

I said little during our family debates. The plight of Mr. Benjamin's daughter was a real-life parable to me. While I truly valued Jesus's message of love, I believed that her father's inflexible piety and interminable scripture lessons hadn't provided any clues about how to navigate life. She was, as was I, a gawky teenager who desperately wanted to belong and respond to a boy who showed interest in her. I noticed that the church, my family, and the community were eager to shun her for breaking a rule when she desperately needed exactly the kind of acceptance Jesus talked about.

Thus, Christianity had failed its test for me, and I happily left it behind for many years. To my father's regret, my church experience became the basis of a lifelong curiosity and quest into the many forms of spirit, including Buddhism and other indigenous faiths. My exploration of an ancient Mayan tradition in the purple hills of New Mexico forced me to look into myself in a radically different way and was directly responsible for my choice to leave my marriage. My search continues to this day.

Because of my fervent spiritual pursuits, my family's multigenerational dedication to Christ, and my own countless prayers, I believed God would keep up her end of the deal and allow my marriage to remain intact. Life and the divine, however, had another plan. I was to have a direct experience of the Buddhist notion of impermanence, destroying everything I held onto so tightly, making a mockery of what I cared about the most.

Chapter 3

Enmeshed in my palette of beliefs was—I am sorry to say—more than a droplet of arrogance, a hefty dose of divine entitlement, and a colossal mass of rigidity. The teachings of the church were simple and clear, resembling an algebraic equation: Jesus equals salvation. Rejecting him or defying the commandments meant hell. It taught me that life has few alternatives, and it's best to hang onto the most popular ones with the same strength I had held on to my mattress that morning long ago.

No place was this clearer than in my relationship to the home John and I bought in 1998 in preparation for starting a family. It was a two-story stucco house with a dingy grayish exterior. Four vertical, brown planks were intended to convey a stylish Tudor motif. Instead, the earthy boards quit halfway down the facade as two windows awkwardly flanked the corners.

"It looks like a walleye," a decorator said.

I insisted that we completely remodel the house for a hefty sum, although John had no interest in home improvement. Since the fifties, his family had owned a cabin in northern Minnesota without electricity or plumbing. Its bonus asset was a 1958 camper whose primary asset was rat poison to keep the winter creatures from eating the red plastic upholstery. Luxury was neither a need nor a want for him.

The whole modeling project was, in fact, a very expensive olive branch after a disagreement regarding misspent funds. The residential facelift was John's contrite method of making amends for his role, as well as serving as a hopeful strategy to reignite our connection. He drew countless project sketches, one of which expanded a kitchen desk to provide more room and flexibility. I had rejected all of them, again insisting on an outside vendor for a neutral, "better" opinion.

The construction crew arrived on a blustery morning in late March. As the four workmen entered the foyer, the three of us stood in an excited tight clump to greet them, grinning like winners of a million-dollar lottery. Our daughter, Jenna, and her six-year-old friends painted a mural on a wall destined for demolition. Using garbage bags as paint aprons, they covered the doomed plaster with brilliant blue and orange pictures of rainbows and happy dogs. The next day, the crew's sledgehammers and crowbars noisily reduced their giant easel to a pile of dusty plasterboard and bent nails.

By the end of the project, the cramped alley kitchen became an open, light-filled space flanked by sparkling cabinets lining the kitchen walls surrounding a large island. The living room gained a maple fireplace with green granite trim. Patio doors replaced the dingy, undersized windows, allowing the backyard's grass and trees to form a pastoral backdrop for meals. The ridiculous pseudo-Tudor exterior was removed and two windows were added, creating a sense of balance and taste to the façade.

The day the kitchen was functional, I invited the neighbors over. They nodded with satisfaction at the teal Corian counters, the numerous cabinets, the slide-out pantry, and the French-style crank-out windows. I didn't even try to hide my pride. Puffed up with happiness, I was unaware that I had again unwittingly contributed to the portrait of domestic perfection I so coveted.

The night after the workmen left, John and I sat in front of our new fireplace taking in the welcoming flames. He answered me sharply when I asked him about finalizing dates for a friend's dinner.

"What's wrong?" I asked.

He sat up stiffly. "Why wouldn't you let me use my designs?"

"Well," I said shifting, "I wanted someone neutral to advise us who did this all the time. I thought we would get a better result."

"Oh," he said, sarcastically. "And that's why you can't even fit a piece of paper on the kitchen desk?"

He was right. I had rejected his ideas because I hadn't liked his tone. The kitchen desk was now so narrow, a letter-sized sheet of paper wouldn't fit. I was quiet for a minute, then said, "You aren't very open to suggestions. You get angry."

He got up and went to the sink for a glass of water, saying, "I've got work to do in the office."

It should have been a nice night, a time to celebrate. I told myself how lucky I was. I had what I wanted: a great kid, a husband who was a good provider, if a bit hard to live with, and now a fabulous house, which he had supported me in remodeling, though he was a bit crabby. I congratulated myself for triumphantly insisting upon and directing the home renewal, and achieving the visible approval from the neighbors.

Yet the queasy sensation in my stomach argued with my rational certainty that everything was fine. I walked into my new kitchen and opened the brand-new cabinets, admiring how easily they opened and closed. I took out a jar of peanut butter and a bag of chips. I watched an episode of a serial drama on the sofa and soon slipped into bed alone. After an hour of restless wakefulness, I took a pill, shutting out any concerns of the moment.

Chapter 4

I have heard several women speak of a moment of uncomfortable doubt about their marriage that they wanted to ignore. In my thirties, I attended a wedding and noticed the groom winking at a guest in a low-cut, satin cocktail dress; she bore a strong resemblance to a magazine cover model. The bride, looking adoringly at her new husband from across the room, also noticed it. Years later, she reported that she had felt a shock resembling a dog recoiling from an electric fence. With considerable force, she spent years quelling her emerging intuition and its warning of impending danger. Listening to it would mean admitting she had made a bad choice while robbing her of the sweetness of a loving though flawed partner. In her desire for self-protection, she chose denial as her best strategy.

This phenomenon of smothering one's own voice is all too familiar. My assumption and fervent hope was that marriage would bring me out of my own pain, distrust, and sense of abandonment, providing a loving, healing connection without effort. Like the bride who witnessed the wink at the wedding, I naively assumed that the foreboding background sounds would disappear with time. I knew early on that if I started listening to the troubling ache inside, I'd be opening a chest of demons I did not want to face. The more strongly I felt conflicted about my relationship, the harder I insisted that I was imagining my own unhappiness.

Once I finally made my decision to dismantle my marriage, I learned that what appeared to be minor emotional blips were actually a cry for help. My heart uttered a sincere and authentic voice. Feelings that presented themselves as wrenching, sad, shocking, and puzzling were reflecting a knowledge that had always been there—a kind of self-authority of the soul that was struggling to make its way to the surface.

My arrogant and naive notion was that God wouldn't do this to me. After a childhood marked by a fire-and-brimstone grandma and a pair of battling and unprepared parents, I believed that I had earned stability, happiness, companionship, contentment, and relief. In what I see now as an intentionally ignorant and inexperienced mind, I assumed life would support my fervent desire and give me a carefree marriage in perpetuity. I was willing to put in the effort, but I never even considered that the outcome was anything but guaranteed—with me as the unquestioned victor.

It is at times like this that the great spirit roars with laughter, a notion that we find unimaginably cruel but is, actually, the whisper of the mercy and challenge of being human.

Chapter 5

In 2003, ten years into my marriage, the solo nights and emotional paper cuts drove me to seek a therapist on my own.

Carol's office was in a white two-story home where she lived with her husband. Built in the twenties by a lumber baron, the house boasted impressive Ionic columns on a street lined with towering maples flourishing in the hot summer sun. I walked across the spacious porch past oversized oval windows into the foyer. As I stood in the welcoming living room with a coved ceiling, I took in the carved elephants that sat on understated teak end tables flanking a generous couch. I entered her office and settled myself on a deep beige armchair next to a stack of cozy afghans.

Dressed in a simple lavender smock and wearing gold teardrop earrings, Carol was quiet as I described recent tension between my husband and me as we reviewed our finances.

"He raised his voice when I asked for more explanation about one of the amounts. When I asked him what was so upsetting, he tapped his finger on a spreadsheet line and said, 'Just look at this line. It's right there. Just look at it!'

"I stared at the line of figures, trying hard to see what was so obvious to him. I still didn't understand and was afraid to admit it, but I told him it still made no sense to me. He kept rolling his eyes as I asked him to please explain it again. He repeated: 'Just look at the left column and then the total on the right.'

"My brain got foggier and foggier and the numbers started swimming in front of me. Finally I stood up and told him I couldn't deal with it. He looked surprised but didn't say anything as I headed out into a whirling winter storm. I wanted to get away from him so badly! I kept walking even though the snow was higher than my boots and the ice kept stinging my face."

Taking notes, Carol was unruffled by my tears. She responded by reading a story about a mythical selkie who lost her skin. She clearly thought the myth would comfort me, but instead it sparked alarm. To me, if the price of recovering her skin was the loss of her partner, such a bounty was unacceptably high.

By the third visit, Carol informed me she was moving. With no "For Sale" sign in front of the house, her sad eyes told the story. She was making the transition alone. Our next visit was in her new home, set in a far more modest neighborhood. The small one-story dwelling with its two cramped bedrooms resembled my first home. She transformed one of them into her office with whimsical oil paintings, beeswax candles, an easy chair covered by a furry fleece, and a sensual female nude.

Sitting in her newly designed space, I related a recent visit to a restaurant with John. I sat awkwardly across from him over stiff breadsticks and a checkered red tablecloth. I had found myself hunting in vain for a topic other than home repair to discuss.

"Just notice," she said. I waited for her to say something else. Instead, she gazed evenly at me, as I focused on her spidery dream catcher earrings. I sat waiting for the tension in the room to lessen. The alabaster statue of a woman calmly carrying water on the table seemed to mock me with an unspoken knowledge.

I finally said impatiently, "Notice what? How miserable I feel?"

"Just notice," she repeated, smiling peacefully.

I had learned to expect this kind of noncommittal statement. Part of me longed for an answer that would give me something decisive to do: a simple plan, action, or strategy that would help me repair my failing marriage and mend my yearning heart.

Yet another part of me was relieved. Her suggestion of such nonjudgmental observation was far better than the dreaded pronouncement from an authority figure that my marriage should end. My unconscious, foreboding knowledge of an inevitable divorce lurked ominously beneath the turmoil I felt. Because I was convinced that I did not have the emotional or economic resources to face such an ordeal, I allowed myself to be satisfied with her gentle command.

When else did I notice? At a Bonnie Raitt concert, I "noticed" a couple get up to dance spontaneously. The wicked look in their eyes was taunting and sensual as the man grabbed his partner and held her, balancing playfulness with enough force to be sexy, yet soft enough to be seductively inviting. I gazed at them as if they were foreigners, but in fact I was the alien, planets away from what I thought I had chosen. Fun? Desire? With him? Laughing together? I honestly didn't know what it felt like.

At home one night, I wandered in the upstairs hallway in my flannel nightgown, noticing my perpetual solitude. Hadn't we talked about this? Wasn't he going to join me at bedtime? I looked at the pictures of my niece's wedding at Lake Tahoe covering the wall. She held her bouquet jubilantly high in the air with the sparkling beach in the background. I reproached myself as I looked at the incomplete photo display that ended by my daughter's room. I had vowed to create a family gallery but quit halfway. As I stood there, I felt a sensation that would have been panic if it hadn't been so familiar. Like a ping-pong ball, I bounced between annoyance at my own petty decorating failure and a subtle but powerful depth of unease.

After another urge from Carol to notice, I leaned forward over the amber candle flame and asked, "Why don't you want me to get a divorce?"

A veteran of two failed marriages, she responded without hesitation, "I don't want you to go through that kind of pain."

Her response stopped me, and I found myself surprised and grateful to her simultaneously. At least she wasn't telling me to leave. But what was I experiencing now if not pain? At least I was avoiding a major disruption in my life, and could count on my own proven methods of dulling my familiar torment. John's keen support increased my confusion as he funded my personal growth efforts without complaint and consistently managed the house. Still, those acts did not remedy the lack of connection and an often desperate desire for closeness. A handful of almonds or a flaky chocolate-filled croissant provided consistent though fleeting comfort. To the outside world, I appeared content.

So I continued to "notice" for almost a decade as my misery deepened, like radon silently wafting between the rafters of a musty basement. The slights, hurtful jabs, and lengthening silences expanded, exploded, and then disappeared from immediate memory. As the offending incidents receded into the past, I could pretend they were only a disturbing and meaningless dream.

Chapter 6

Now, at the end of my twenty-year marriage, I awoke to my self-imposed delusion. I saw a vacant and frightening future ahead, stripped of my cherished identity as a wife. Unwillingly, I began to adjust to the reality of life as a single woman. I made slow progress, feeling like a horse navigating a stony mountain path, careful not to break a leg. I knew I needed a new therapist who, unlike Carol, was willing to look at my dismembered life head-on and help me grow into a different place without sparing me from ugly and inconvenient truths. I looked for one with the same urgency I'd used to find an expert plumber after the toilet overflowed.

I found Clarice, a kind-looking, fifty-something white woman with light-colored curly hair. She wore an informal linen blouse and flowered skirt to our first session in an early twentieth-century house that had been converted to offices. When I asked her about her counseling philosophy, she said the central theme was the client relationship.

I don't need a friend, I thought. *I need a lobotomy so I can get through this.* I proceeded to lay out my plight in earnest.

"I've been married for twenty years, and it is over. I counted on him for everything. I got married at forty-two, and it seemed so perfect. We have a teenager in the house. It kills me to do this, but I just can't go on. I worked so hard, and I just couldn't get him to change. This was never supposed to happen to me. We were in therapy together for twelve years. I know I have to leave, but my parents were divorced and . . ." I paused and wiped my nose.

As I described my stance of unique and prideful misfortune, she paused, looked at me, and responded with a story.

"One of the women in my suicide support group said all she wanted was to write in block letters on her forehead: 'My mother killed herself.'"

This set me back. I wondered silently: *Is that worse than what had happened to me?* I was genuinely unsure. I could acknowledge that the woman's experience was undeniably tragic, but it did not involve the disintegration of her nuclear family, the people she lived with every day, and the person she slept with. That made her plight seem not quite so bad.

But I did resonate with one point the therapist was making: that woman wanted everybody to know what had happened to her. Her mother's suicide was having a catastrophic impact on her life as she roamed a world now empty of the person who had given her life dimension and meaning. Her calamitous misfortune served as an identity card with the same authority as a passport offers proof of citizenship. Now that she was a resident in the land of excruciating grief, her entire existence was defined by her mother's death. She preferred to live in its defining shadow, an outstandingly visible victim of loss.

That I understood. Everything had been altered for that woman, and, like her, I wanted everyone to know. I yearned for attention and recognition for my own calamitous misfortune.

I looked at the therapist and haltingly told her of the time my three-year-old daughter gleefully looked at her recessed belly button and said with wonder, "You have an innie and daddy has an innie. We're an innie family!"

"I can't live with myself that I've destroyed this for her," I said, "us being together. And her being so happy."

"Tell me about your early life," she said.

"I had bouts of depression in college," I said. "I went to a counselor once when I felt like the world was crushing me. He asked questions about my friends and tried to be nice, but really, he scared me. The counselor sent the dorm mother after me and I avoided her." As I laid out my story, I thought: Wasn't all this worth a little attention?

The therapist sat quietly with a steady gaze. Uncomfortable with the silence, I spoke up: "I just can't imagine being worse off." I waited for affirmation and agreement. I was thoroughly convinced that chronic illness, poverty, and loss of job were tiny things. I had lost my mate, who, though flawed, had been my source of balance and support. I was only interested in stopping the flow of grief and escaping my agony. I wanted her to fix it.

As I waited for her to speak, I thought of the woman in the support group who wanted her mother's suicide announcement embedded in her flesh. I mused about crafting my own eye-catching sign on my face. Should it be a bright red skull to mirror the lifeblood I was losing? A bouquet of dead lilacs showing how a once sweet fragrance was now dried up and lifeless? What story did I want to tell? It was not a simple tale of affection diminishing over time and growing apart. It contained elements of anger, gratitude, disappointment, joy, awakening, denial, and—most painful—growth.

As the notion rattled around in my head, I suddenly knew my tattoo should be Shiva, the colorful, trident-bearing, Hindu god of destruction. Often depicted with a peaceful smile and a snake around his neck, he is known for destroying things when they no longer serve, often in a grand gesture of devastation. It must have been him, I thought, who was responsible for banishing what I counted on the most. Perhaps the tattoo could tell the story in a concise and powerful way, so I wouldn't have to face the world and report this shameful news. The inky symbol could help me avoid the comments of another mom on the athletic field who made hushed, disparaging remarks about the disruptive behavior of kids from "broken homes." I also believed I could have avoided a teary scene during my recent interview with two young and well-meaning financial planners. Yes, I thought, a tattoo could thwart unwanted criticism and symbolize past events, allowing me to speak only when I chose.

She then asked, "What was your everyday life like? What patterns existed between the two of you?"

I told her about my ongoing attempts to run a cheerful and festive household, especially around holidays. One year, I participated in a Christmas cookie exchange. I simultaneously produced three baked goods: a crescent shortbread cookie dipped in bittersweet chocolate with marmalade nestled in a thumbprint; a yuletide loaf festooned with brandy sauce; and triangular molasses-based cookies with red noses, mimicking Rudolph the Red-Nosed Reindeer.

The kitchen island, the size of a small car, was covered with cookie sheets in a disheveled stack. Dented from years of snappy bake offs, the pans hosted tiny bits of blackened grease in their crevices. The stovetop had a slippery yellow blotch where I had accidentally smashed an egg as I reached for the cinnamon. A stick of melted butter had overflowed the saucer and spilled onto the floor. I slipped on the greasy spot and performed an awkward gymnastic split, sparking a painful stretch in my piriformis. I held a tray of doughy cookies en route to the oven, so my hands were too full to wipe it up.

John walked through the kitchen and took in the flour dusting the counters, the bowls of sugary batter, and the band of greasy bowls. Then he pulled his jacket out of the closet.

"Did you have to make so many?" he said quietly.

"Of course I do! It's a Minnesota cookie bake! How should I know why they want me to make six dozen?"

He nodded as he reached for a broken reindeer. "You better wipe up that greasy spot. Looks dangerous," he said, munching his cookie as he walked out the door to shovel snow.

The tears continued to flow as I faced Clarice. "There were so many good times," I mourned. "He was there for me in so many ways."

She leaned forward. "You're leading with a broken heart. That doesn't usually happen. Most often women are so angry they didn't get what they want, but you're in a different place."

I nodded and had a glimmer of gratitude. She was seeing something I had been unable to put into words.

Time was up with the therapist. I wanted to tell her about other particularly desperate times: the time when I begged him to come with me to the opera on my birthday, and he left me in the lobby to help a displaced person at a place he volunteered. When he yelled at me in front of the construction workers during the remodel and they stood awkwardly silent. When I was so deep in despair after experiencing his unbridled arrogance, I attended a service at an African Methodist Episcopal Church.

The clergyman had called people to the altar to pray:

"Anyyyyyyything that's wrong—know there is redemption! If there are drugs, Jesus will help! If your child is sick, Jesus will help! If you have lost your faith— have no fear! Jesus is there for you."

That day, I had crept to the altar in desperation. Feeling scared and self-conscious, I knelt on the maroon pillow and folded my hands on the rail. A parishioner came over and gently touched my shoulder. I remembered a verse from the Bible: "I have touched the hem of his garment and his power has made me whole." The weight of hopelessness lifted for that moment, but it did not heal my pervasive anxiety and panic. I still felt I was in a prison with window bars too high to reach.

I kept asking myself, *How would he cope if the marriage ended?* Second to that was a bitter inquiry about how I could continue to live with such an intense feeling of helplessness and separation from my spouse, God, and, worst of all, myself.

But we were done for the day. Although she had been somewhat empathetic, I still felt that I had not received the wholehearted sympathy I deserved for my reduced status and newfound, though shaky, commitment to myself.

As I obsessed over my own journey, it did not occur to me that I was self-centered or narcissistic. The mental capacity to reflect was totally unavailable. The ballad of misery and self-pity played with the strength of a Verdi aria. Puffed up with self-justification, I took my place as the principal diva of tragedy as my new life began. Other days, I felt like the lead crash test dummy in the General Motors test line.

On a balmy May afternoon in the week following my therapy appointment, a friend and I rented a fifties-style Alumacraft canoe at a nearby lake. The two of us dragged the sturdy, dented vessel into the lake as my bare ankles sank into the tepid sand.

We took our places on the hard metal seats and made some half-hearted strokes, steering out of the swimming area marked by blue fiberglass ropes and red buoys. We made our way over to a marshy area, away from the growing number of paddleboats and attentive moms watching their diaper-clad children. Under any other circumstances, the warm sun, green grasses, and cattails would have been a picture of unbridled joy after a Minnesota winter.

As my friend steered our craft ahead, I thought about the kitchen scene I had described to Clarice. I could see now how I had created a frantic tornado to accomplish daily tasks only I thought were urgent. Starting projects late enough to ignite a crisis became a dependable coping mechanism, masking what I felt inside. Despite my vehement tirades about feminism, masquerading as a 1950s homemaker with my fingers stuck in cookie dough was a lot easier than crafting a new identity and facing my discontent.

The images of my culinary frenzy faded as I looked at the burgeoning spring growth. While we floated quietly near the bank, other thoughts emerged that had been buried as deeply as the roots of the sheltering oak trees. I saw my Olympic ability to abandon myself as an unintentional effort to demolish my marriage. Oblivious to my well-being, I had disowned my own power and ability to make my own choices. I began to see that a huge majority of the beliefs and behaviors that destroyed my marriage were created by none other than me. I now saw that I had to reconstruct myself and deal with why I had chosen to stay so long in a life-diminishing situation. Instead of pulling a few unsightly weeds, I was going to have to redesign my entire landscape.

I turned to my friend and said, "I'm Rosie the Riveter of codependence."

She smiled, dragging her fingers in the water. "You aren't alone."

Sighing, I draped my legs over the gunwales into the coolness of the lake. Just weeks after our marriage ended, I could see how deeply I had participated in destroying the vessel that held us, which was nowhere near as sturdy as this canoe. Gratefully, I was equally blessed with an acorn seed of divinity and a deep knowing that things were going to be all right over the long run.

Even with that prescient knowledge, I knew that the pathway ahead contained hidden traps. Yet I held a portion of faith that pulled me along the journey, giving me uncanny and unexpected endurance. Off I went, naked, vulnerable, and whimpering. It would be years before I would be able to understand how deeply I had chosen to be a victim, costing me years as I avoided my own strength and agency. Like a panicked stallion, I was paralyzed in quicksand and had only a bare sense of hope to go forward. It would have to be enough.

Chapter 7

As time went by during that spring of 2013, I turned to the river: my solace, friend, and savior.

Years before, in happier times, I had walked the four blocks in the winter to the river boulevard, meandering through a thoroughfare of weeping willows, maples, and quiet, hundred-year-old homes, praying along the way. I gazed at the frozen Mississippi, still mighty in its icy state. The solid water moaned, creaked, and yawned, its frosty cracks like giant diamonds. In my mind's eye, there appeared a series of beings, several stories high. They walked along with me atop the solid cold surface, honoring me with their presence, confirming that my pursuit of spirit was clear and true and would serve me in good stead. Equally important was the knowledge that they would be there whenever I needed them.

Now, in my bereft state, I stumbled down to the river's banks and retreated to a parallel earthen trail hidden by clumps of buckthorn and sumac. This path became my refuge as I ran crying into the trees as often as five times a day.

Sacred mother life, comfort me at this moment! In her silent arms, she would reach out, harboring me with the highest level of compassion for the lot of being human, of loving and having it end, of the courage it took to carry on, of stepping out and not seeing anything or anyone to hold me. The earth was my anchor as I summoned the resolve to continue when everything I had counted on had fallen apart.

Just one more step. Take it, I said to myself as I walked. A friend's adage played back continuously: "What do you do when you are in hell?"

"Keep going," was the wise response.

After a few minutes, the turbulence in my body faded. I knew that the great spirit saw my sorrow and I began to see that I was never alone.

Those moments of the greatest desolation became the gateways to a deep knowledge that I was part of the whole.

One day I discovered my usual place of prayer by the water was cordoned off with yellow police tape. Pictures of a family were taped to a protective hurricane fence. Apparently, a man had fallen into the river's ravine and suffered fatal injuries. The sense of grief was as palpable as the gray-green boulders lining the limestone cliffs. Focused on my own shock, I felt no compassion, only a knowledge that I wasn't the only one suffering loss that day.

On another day, I saw a clear image of myself floating high over the gorge where the Mississippi was flowing. I heard a message: "The resources are always there." It was calming and centering. This phrase became a constant friend.

More assurance appeared from a surprising place. In the bosom of cosmic humor, I kept accidentally pulling up the video of Bobby McFerrin's tune "Don't Worry Be Happy." With uncanny regularity, I saw the singer and his entourage boogying across the stage with chartreuse polyester pants and dreadlocks hanging down to their shoulders. The hapless comic characters danced across the screen, cheerfully singing about their woeful fate of being evicted and penniless. Even though I fiercely maintained my place in the high court of doom, I couldn't help but smile as they bopped in time with the music, reducing any hardship to an endearing comedy, clinking xylophone notes in the undercurrent of life.

I was inspired by their catchy tune as the figures jumped back and forth from catastrophic failure to heartfelt merriment. I imagined them hopping from one piece of ice to another in my stretch of the Mississippi River. Although they could choose to stand on the shore, they knew that life in its full expression was in the river, leaping and moving forward on a perilous piece of ice, not cowering in a warm spot to wait for spring. I was starting to realize that I never knew what the ice would do: get trapped in a rapid and pitch forward unpredictably? Crash into a tree and leave the victim with a broken leg? Or host a mirth-filled, bouncy ride? Any assurance that I could predict the outcome was sheer illusion.

I came to feel as if I were standing naked in a fire tower in northern Minnesota's boreal forest, touched by a breeze that was both bracing and inviting. There was a refreshing exuberance in not having to pretend I knew the answer. I was learning in my own wobbly way to adjust to my erratic bandwidth of emotions while growing muscles to deal with another unwelcome wave of despair. As Rumi says, "Every guest brings a piece of life that we need, and if we refuse to let one in the door, who knows what we have missed?"

Meanwhile, my soon to be ex-husband, daughter, and I had scheduled a family trip in June to visit Ecuador, where my brother, Phil, was a medical missionary. John and I agreed not to tell our daughter about the divorce until we returned home. We knew it was going to be a trip we remembered forever, and we would not sully it with the life-changing shadow of her parents splitting up.

Phil picked up the three of us at the Quito airport in his white van with multiple food stains on the seats and a plastic Pepsi cup on the floor. A lanky six-foot-four, he grabbed our luggage with a big smile, and we sped off to a modest guesthouse protected by a cement block wall with rolls of barbed wire on top. We were welcomed by my sister-in-law and their four red-headed boys aged four to ten with hugs all around, especially for our sixteen-year-old daughter, who was revered like a big sister.

"Jenna!" Each one shouted, pulling on her arms and shirt to grab her attention. They pushed her to the floor and took turns jumping on her as their giggles mounted. The smallest one took her hand to proudly show off the playroom upstairs set up with his latest Lego invention.

"Wow, to see my family on my turf, in my place, is really something," Phil said with a grin that matched his lanky stature. I had never seen my confident doctor brother show such raw gratitude and humility.

We all nodded, and a sweet silence settled over us. I was awed at his fulfillment of his childhood dream: using his skills and faith to heal others in a country that needed medical support. Although we had visited one another sporadically during his six-year tenure in Ecuador, I always had a sense of vague unfamiliarity and distance about his calling. At that moment, standing on the aging laminated floors and leaning against the gray Formica counters, we were united in the joy of a special family reunion in his adopted land.

The trip was also a welcome vacation from my tormented mind. For the coming weeks, I could dissolve in the contented cloud of my brother's tight-knit family, pretending all was well, ignoring the secret that my family would soon be torn asunder. In addition, I could satisfy my desire for an extraordinary excursion. John, Jenna, and I would spend four days in the deep Amazon jungle at an award-winning ecolodge hosted by the Achuar tribe.

The three of us took off with great anticipation in a small, two-engine plane from a little town on the edge of the rainforest. A series of dents on the craft's bare metal body peeked through a battered coat of beige and blue paint. Inside, it resembled a shabby movie theater, with twelve lumpy olive seats and one bright yellow one. With relief, I noticed the propeller was intact.

Prone to unnecessary worry, I literally rewrote my will prior to the trip. I was convinced I would be found dead on the floor of the Amazon jungle, my main heir along with me. Laden with such heightened anxiety, I was surprised by the gentle ascent as I gazed out on the vast, verdant landscape beneath me in what was one of the calmest plane rides I had ever had.

After an hour in the air, we descended onto a densely packed dirt airstrip created by the hands of the local people. Although there was nothing resembling a terminal, we were met by a small group of villagers. The women were dressed in brightly colored, ankle-length traditional fabrics and necklaces with multiple strings of tiny red and blue beads. Several small children clung to their mothers' knees while others sneaked shy glances at us.

Next to the group of women stood two men. Arturo, our English-speaking Ecuadorian guide, wore glasses, shorts, and a white shirt. Octavio stood next to him in a plain blue shirt, his face tattooed with black lines meant to protect him from harm while moving through the rainforest. A black-and-red ring sat on his head, a symbol of his membership in the Achuar tribe.

Arturo and Octavio carried the baggage as our group left the ocher-colored airstrip and walked down a path. We stepped onto a generous boardwalk suspended some fifteen feet above a serene body of water flowing beneath our feet. Rich foliage surrounded us on both sides. In this tranquil setting, it was hard to believe this was the legendary Amazon, home of piranhas, deadly snakes, and countless dramas of terror and courage, both real and fictitious.

The main lodge boasted a majestic vaulted ceiling supported by beams from local palm trees. A thatched roof formed the ceiling, its leafy strands fastened together with what looked like a plant-based twine. The effect was an imposing open-air structure crafted in traditional Achuar style with gleaming wooden floors; grasses, trees, and water were visible on three sides. One end had a dining hall where we would eat photo-worthy meals of braised pork, spicy ceviche, and local vegetables topped with edible flowers.

Our lodge sat in a group of huts connected by a winding path resembling branches jutting out from a tree trunk. Also crafted in the local tradition, the huts exuded a keen elegance. Our cozy dwelling had a jungle hammock, an ornate bed with a colorful, embroidered quilt, and a single bed with an appealing comforter. A smaller version of the main lodge, it had plaster walls that met a more modest but beautifully arched ceiling. The bathroom held sleek modern fixtures and was painted a restful peach color. Local women with carts full of toilet paper and soaps quietly roamed the area in their ankle-length dresses.

Our mood was high as we claimed our sumptuous lodgings. Jenna immediately claimed the hammock, swinging it with the whimsical energy of a newfound toy.

After we settled in, Arturo led us down to a riverbank with double kayaks resting on a muddy shore. Unlike the plane, they were a vibrant green and seemed new. I cringed internally as Arturo automatically paired John and me together. But, I reasoned, no one had any reason to assume our partnership was in question.

John and I had spent lots of time in boats together, most often at his family cabin in northern Minnesota. Canoeing was one of my few memories of unsullied happiness with him. Those lake experiences became staves of the basket that had held us together for so many years, but the memories were not without rancor. My mind flashed on a common scene involving boarding the canoe up north.

"Hold on," he said. "No, not there," he said impatiently. "Move your hands farther up. Straighten up to keep your balance."

I looked at him with disdain. "I'm not an idiot."

On this occasion in Ecuador, thousands of miles from Minnesota, he said nothing at all as we settled ourselves into the kayak. He manned the stern the way he always had, silent and dependable as he compensated for my erratic paddling by making slight adjustments with each stroke. It was one task he never complained about. Maybe he was also remembering our many happy times in tiny maritime crafts. As my feet rested on the wet kayak floor, I felt sad in the knowledge that this simple joyful activity was coming to an end.

Floating slowly down the river, I noted that the dozens of trees didn't look so different from the deciduous ones in the upper Midwest. I could see that the forest contained differing heights and trunk sizes holding oddly shaped leaves. Each one had its own personality. Some of the fronds were tiny and crowded, creating a cluster on a small stem that ended in an imposing, feathery mass. Others were skinny and tall with bumps and spikes on their trunks, their leaves almost resembling California palm trees, but here they were bigger, wider, and wilder.

We heard bird calls, and Octavio identified the opal-crowned tanager and the green honeycreeper. Eventually we pulled the boat up on a beach and made our way onto a hidden path in the crowded jungle floor. Octavio pointed out vines that were woven together and used for rope as we had seen at the lodge. He helped us in our clumsy efforts to braid them.

He then showed us the kapok tree with its whitish bark and majestic branches that stretched over the forest canopy. His daughter had done her rite of passage there, staying awake all night to listen to her ancestors' voices and learn her unique purpose. The kapok's trunk was more than thirty feet wide and rose over a hundred feet high, supported by numerous columns of wood that reached out like flying buttresses to grasp the forest's floor, more closely resembling a medieval cathedral than a woody jungle being. The kapok's bark reminded me of my grandmother's wrinkly face; its cracks and fissures filled with a fuzzy greenish moss providing welcome terrain for tiny ants. The tree's size, elegance, and sacred purpose brought us to a state of awe-filled silence.

Arturo continued to point out life forms that existed only in this place: a nocturnal frog with a gossamer skin too frail for sunlight. He then pointed very high at a neighboring tree.

"Spider monkeys," he said.

With considerable effort I peered through my binoculars, and located three identical monkeys calmly staring back at us. Their eyes were surrounded with white as if they were dressed for Halloween, their heads looking like coconuts with white ears.

The resort offered an overnight excursion to a nearby Achuar village, which meant abandoning our comfortable hut. John declined to come, so my daughter and I set off in a large canoe, with Arturo and Octavio paddling cheerfully. We spent the night in an open-air plaza, a far cry from the resort's pampered setting. Under a thatched roof the size of a city block and protected only by mosquito nets, we put down woven mats for our night's sleep.

We then visited an elder's home, with its walls of woven leaves and a dirt floor. Our host sat quietly and unhurried in the receding light, focused on the basket he was weaving. His fingers slowly pulled the parched grass together into a tight pattern, creating a vessel that would haul water and countless other items for daily use. Octavio translated the villager's Achuar words to Spanish, and Arturo then translated them into English.

In his village, he said slowly, health was the number one concern. A villager could die from a snakebite. I thought immediately of my brother, a short plane ride away, who had all the resources to help. However, it could well have been one thousand miles with the lack of available transport. The elder also explained about the oil companies that, with increasing insistence, were using their influence to pressure the tribe into surrendering its land for drilling.

The older man continued slowly pulling a wayward thread through the half-finished vessel. As he spoke, the departing sun cast deepening shadows. No electricity brightened his home or anything else in the village. Silence, the sister of darkness, formed a deepening mist with no noise of any kind: no cars, planes, bikes, or throngs of people. The other-worldly obscurity and quiet produced a sensation of both mystery and welcome with none of the distractions that would normally rob us of our connection to the earth and one another.

I was acutely conscious that we were privileged people allowed to experience this ancient landscape in luxury and that we would leave the next day. We returned to our village home in the plaza, feasted on gourmet food, and slept fitfully on the ground, sheltered by the gauze netting. In the morning, we joined the villagers at 4:00 a.m. for their daily ritual of drinking ayahuasca. In the predawn hours, two villagers tended a wood fire with a large iron pot suspended over it. In the velvet darkness, our group sat on a log alongside a few village men. The fire tenders put hot water into a pitcher with spoonfuls of the powerful herb. They then poured the mixture into a communal cup, which was passed to each of us. As I took a sip, I remembered its purpose: to wash away dreams and allow the community to start the day afresh. Perhaps, I hoped, it would provide a new vision for me as well.

Shortly thereafter, I squatted behind a hut as my digestive system produced a memorable case of diarrhea. In nature's dependable rhythm of cycles, my body was releasing toxins in a way my mind could not. We departed shortly thereafter, after purchasing numerous bowls in striking orange and brown shades sold by a timid group of village women.

What I remember most is not the perfectly manicured and colorful rooms, the food, or the treasured time with the Achuar people. It was the jungle itself. As we walked down the boardwalk across the river into a garden of seemingly ordinary plants, Arturo explained, "There are ten thousand herbs here for healing. Ten thousand."

This knowledge was a gift. I began to sneak off to a nearby patch of jungle several times a day. I gazed at the rubber and palm trees and watched the insects scurry about, seeking the magical root or leaf that would mend my broken heart.

"Heal me!" I screamed out of earshot of the huts. For a few minutes I would feel better. The sickness in my stomach would disappear, and the Earth itself would quietly sit, undisturbed by my pleading tirade.

As we departed the Ecuadorian jungle in the same ramshackle small plane, we were immediately engulfed in a cloud as thick as a stuffed bag of cotton wool, in what appeared to be a seemingly solid, impenetrable force. Terrified, I imagined my impending death on the jungle's grassy floor. Just as suddenly the sky cleared completely, and we were met with a stunning view of palm trees and ribbons of serpentine rivers surrounded by a puffy blue heaven.

The significance of the sudden clearing wasn't lost on me. The thickest fog can vanish in a second, dissolving doubt, fear, and uncertainty both inside one's psyche and in the physical world. I relaxed and sat back, allowing myself a moment to sit on a wispy breath of God, knowing there would be plenty of time to worry ahead.

36

Chapter 8

Six weeks later, on an idyllic July day, I sat on the scruffy grass in my backyard, surrounded by a circle of stones embedded in the ground, mimicking a medicine wheel. In this place, I could welcome my best self. Today, we would tell our daughter our marriage was over.

I looked at the earth-colored stains on my shorts. I listened to the song of the cardinal nesting in the poplar tree, calling its mate. I gazed at the tall, straight row of cedars in the neighbor's yard. As I saw John and Jenna walk into the kitchen through the window, I ignored the nausea in my abdomen, stood up, and walked inside. As the three of us leaned on the counter that had been the source of so many celebrations, John read directly from the script whose wording we had agreed on, which horrified me. It was as if he was an actor who hadn't bothered to learn his lines for opening night. I gave myself a moment to hide my annoyance before I gazed at Jenna.

There was little outward reaction from her as we shared the secret we had hidden for more than two months. I was silent as I witnessed my own bitter release of my commitment to keep the family intact for her. This was an act to save myself.

We spent the rest of the day cleaning out the basement together, sorting old magazines, outworn toys, and broken tools. We got dinner at Target and watched a romantic comedy on the couch together, with no conversation about our momentous pronouncement that would change us forever. The setting sun blessedly brought a quiet end to the day, saying farewell to our severed dream and leaving behind three silent, lonely, and wounded hearts. It was the saddest day of my life.

Chapter 9

Two weeks after breaking the news to our daughter, we made an unanticipated family trip to our cabin in northern Minnesota. My husband and I needed to sign legal papers, and my daughter wanted to avoid the months-long wait in the metro area for her driving test.

My first visit to the cabin had taken place one month after John and I started dating. It was a charmed trip in 1991 to a township fifteen miles from the legendary and pristine Boundary Waters Canoe Area. We had to stop the car to avoid hitting nine eight-point bucks that stood oblivious in the middle of the road no more than a mile from the turnoff. John said with surprise that he had never seen such a sight in the thirty years he had been making the journey. It was an omen of good fortune as the cabin became a steadfast fixture in my life for twenty years.

The times at the cabin had always been sweet. We slept in the small travel trailer that sat in the gravel driveway next to the cabin. John and I occupied the double bed while our daughter took over the cozy space created from collapsing the kitchen table. With no electricity, we splashed in the lake, hiked, and sat in a sweltering sauna, creating a closeness unavailable in our urban home. When there was rain, we huddled together and read or went into town. Past visits had always been marked with a series of predictable pouts from the young lady and complaints of boredom. I would retreat to the deck to read a book while my spouse ventured out to continue his fight against the spread of the invasive Siberian peashrub.

This visit was starkly different. The three of us played a board game with a sense of deep kindness I had never seen before. Such behavior was unheard of on a beautiful northern Minnesota day, when we would usually be swimming, paddling, or bird-watching. No one criticized one another for a misspelled word, no adolescent complaints about how "You always take too long, Mom!" Instead, it was, "Let me help you with that," including warm-hearted smiles all around, a sincere engagement in the game, and a thoughtful appreciation for one another.

When the game ended, I took a walk in the woods and sat on the ground looking out at the lapping water. I burst into tears. How could I give this up? How could life take away a level of joy and comfort I had worked for all my life?

On the ride home, I became possessed with intense anxiety. I had experienced such symptoms before, following an airplane incident decades earlier. As I contentedly read a spy novel and guzzled a scotch and water, the plane bounced after hitting a pocket of air. After another, bigger drop, the plane went into a free fall of more than one hundred feet. A unified scream of terror filled the aircraft until the vessel stopped abruptly and leveled off. I sat silently, frozen in my seat, panic trapped in my body. Only the death of a dear aunt a year later forced me into the air again.

The abrupt end to my marriage prompted the return of my buried fears on that July day. On that long drive home from the north woods, I became suddenly terrified of high-speed traffic, and I insisted we leave the highway and return via country roads. Passing the boreal tree cover on that summer day, John emerged as the dutiful helpmate, complying with my request. My daughter took the front seat stoically and chose to ignore me, her lips in a scornful frown. I curled up horizontally in the back seat, convinced we could be struck and destroyed at any moment.

To deal with this alarming symptom, I worked with an Eye Movement Desensitization and Reprocessing—EMDR—therapist. A popular therapy with post-traumatic stress patients, the treatment evokes body sensations along with past experiences. The approach pairs unprocessed negative emotions with happy ones, thus providing positive anchors to diminish the impact of traumatic events.

Unlike most therapists I had seen, the EMDR professional actually had a sense of humor. She was a statuesque six feet tall, owning her willowy body with strong measured movements topped by bouncy tipped hair and a ready smile. She presented a snappy energetic presence with a twinkle in her eye. Her fees were also bloody expensive, but she could do an imitation of an arrogant white male that put me into a rare bout of giggles.

With her skilled support, I began to delve into childhood scenes, recalling pivotal memories that felt like disturbing dreams. I sat in the chair, holding the EMDR handles that looked like jumper cables. As I watched a row of lights move back and forth on a bar, listening to a rhythmic beeping sound, I began to tell my story.

•- -•- -•-

When I was seven, I was admitted to a local hospital. It was 1958. Dressed in a pair of pedal pushers and my best T-shirt, I stood with my mother in a foyer resembling a church narthex. I looked up at the nuns in their long habits with my mouth open. I had never stood so close to these formidable black and white figures. Their faces were pressed in on all sides by what looked like a beveled cardboard paper plate. Flowing black headpieces ran down to their hips. Long rosaries hung from their waists with a twisted carving of the martyred Jesus on the cross.

I wanted to ask them why they hurt themselves by smushing their faces, but even at age seven, I knew I wasn't supposed to ask such things. I shivered with the knowledge that I was now under their command.

The oldest one turned to me with a smile.

"Oh," she said, bending over, "we're glad you're here. You look just like my grandniece, Cindy."

I looked down as I clung to my mom, hiding my smile and red face, as another one said, "You know we give kids ice cream when they start getting well. We'll take good care of you. Don't you worry!"

Excited by the prospect, I wondered which kind of ice cream I would get. Their welcome contradicted the tales I had heard about nuns using rulers to strike the knuckles of my Catholic friends. My mother beamed at her partners in crime.

Despite their friendliness, I still cringed at the violent figures hanging from their waists. I remembered my father's tirades about Catholic idolatry. Because of his vehement hatred of "R.C.s," as my dad called them, I knew the hospital was my mother's decision.

I was there because of an unknown malady that was never explained to me. I was led into a ward where I changed into a white hospital gown and climbed into bed. During that first of several hospital stays, I begged my mother not to leave me. She arranged to have a nurse sit next to my bed for the night. I remember looking at the stranger, the light behind her illuminating her signature nurse's hat and bright pink uniform. She looked a bit like an angel as I fell asleep.

When my mom returned the next day, she brought a present wrapped with orange-and-green paper and a crimson ribbon. With money always scarce in our house, gifts were rare, especially ones wrapped with ornate, crinkly bows. Inside was *The Tall Book of Make-Believe*, a precious keepsake I remember to this day. This was the beginning of seeing the rewards of illness and my mother playing a role in its encouragement.

I was familiar with sickness. On our summer vacation earlier that year, I laid awake at my aunt's house in Georgia. I writhed on the bed with stomach pains as I heard the clock tower across the street strike 3:00 a.m. When I told my mom about it the next morning, she headed directly for the bathroom and returned with a red rubber bag connected to a hose and black nozzle. Both parents were convinced that enemas were universal cures for any ailment. Although I hid in a closet to avoid her, I was soon discovered, and spent the afternoon face down with the disgusting contraption doing its duty.

Knowing my mother as I did, I schemed to avoid her next attempt to implement her favorite treatment. I found a pair of scissors and cut the tubing close to the nozzle. My mother looked at me with wounded disappointment when she discovered my calculated mischief. I was rarely more pleased with myself than I was at that moment. I had successfully outsmarted her and her wretched device! Unfortunately, she fixed it with a triumphant expression of glee, holding up the repaired hose like a blue ribbon at the state fair.

Her usual remedy failed to stop my pain, and it became clear that my ailment was actually serious. In the height of a sweltering July summer, I was admitted to a hospital in a small northwestern Georgia town for a severe intestinal disorder. My frightened sister later told me she believed I would die. Whether or not that was true, I do know that my mother received unflattering notoriety among the medical staff.

As she stood over my hospital bed, she said to the doctor, "Aren't you going to give her a shot to make her feel better?"

"No, Mrs. Barton, we've got it handled," he replied firmly in his white smock with a stethoscope around his neck.

"How about an enema?" she inquired hopefully.

Turning to her, he said calmly, "No, that's not the problem."

"A dose of penicillin?" she urged.

Then, in a voice that was teasing, glib, and condescending, he said, "Now, Mama, I just may have to ask you to leave."

Though he was not present, Dad frequently used the story about the doctor's reprimand to condemn my mother's inappropriate, overbearing behavior. For me, it was just another example of the dual nature of her conflicting desire to provide comfort and, with a desire for deluded control, determine what would happen to my body. I will never know how much of her behavior was concern for my well-being and how much a manifestation of her own disease.

The therapist asked, "What did you think about the way she took care of you?"

The question surprised me. "I thought it was just what moms did."

She nodded and I continued.

In April 1959 I was eight years old. I stood in my bedroom and traced the lines of the plywood with my small fingers at our prefab house in New York state. The walls of our home had no paint, wallpaper, or curtains.

I had fled to my room to avoid my mother's constant inquiries about how I was feeling. Now late for school, I dashed into the kitchen, barely sitting down to the bowl of Rice Krispies my mother had poured for me. She smiled at me, and I noticed how perfect her short, curly raven hair was. My father stood with a silent scowl as he walked into the room while attaching his cuff links.

"Do you want a ride?" she asked, with a concerned smile.

Her tone made me suspicious. Although the house was not filled with familiar bursts of temper, there was an invisible tension I had no words for.

"No," I answered shortly, wanting to avoid another monologue about how you had to go to bed when you didn't feel good. I hurriedly gobbled the cereal and grabbed my sweater to leave.

"Are you sure you don't want a ride, honey?" she said cajolingly, hovering over me.

"*No,*" I repeated, as I ran out the door.

I walked quickly down the black pavement toward the school, past the boxy new 1950s houses, determined to be on time for my second-grade class. Before I came to the end of the block, I felt something moving up my throat as painful as the gash on my arm after I had fallen off my bike. I turned and ran back home, hearing my parents' familiar accusatory shouts at each other as soon as I stepped onto the sidewalk leading up to our house.

I intentionally slammed the door after me. They stood across from one another in the living room, their faces distorted with rage. Surprised, Mom turned to me. My father sullenly walked into the kitchen.

"What's the matter?" Mom said, leaning over me.

I said nothing, but plunged into the refuge of her arms unable to explain what I was feeling. I only knew that my only haven was full of cries of mutual accusation coming from the two people I loved most in the world.

She drove me to school in our gray Plymouth station wagon with wooden side panels. The windshield reflected my pink, puffy face back to me. Before I left the car, I put my arms around her like a barnacle, and only reluctantly let go.

"It sounds like there was a lot of conflict in your home. How did you deal with that?" the therapist asked.

"I remember going outside and sitting on a big rock down the hill and crying. I would hide there until I stopped."

She nodded.

A few months before the end of my second-grade year, we moved to a town in New Jersey closer to my father's office in New York. At first, I was excited. Our new home had an oversized dollhouse in the backyard, and I couldn't wait to play there. But when we arrived, I saw that it was weathered and neglected, lacking the magical qualities I so wanted. Green paint was covered with a dirty, moss-like substance. It had no furniture, only empty rooms with rotting pine cones and a few mismatched Lincoln Logs. Instead of creating a rich imaginary world with a new miniature home, I sat alone in the backyard with my treasured baby doll, who wore a pink hat, flowered dress, and tiny plastic shoes. I gazed at the pot-bellied German couple next door who walked their dachshunds past our yard in matching red sweaters, their canine bellies dragging on the ground. The humans smelled strongly of beer, a forbidden substance in my house.

My new teacher, Mrs. Maylor, was an elderly, bent, old-fashioned woman. With wrinkled cheeks, she reminded me more of my grandmother than a teacher. I walked home for lunch alone and scrounged in the kitchen for peanut butter and jelly on Wonder Bread, returning to my class obediently each afternoon.

In our new home, my mother stayed upstairs for long periods, less and less visible during daily routines. She did, however, emerge regularly to make Betty Crocker angel food cake with its colorful confetti flakes. She let me mix the batter with a spoon and carefully guide it into the special tube pan. Close to her warm attentive body, I far preferred that pastime to sitting at a desk and improving my reading in an unfamiliar setting.

With my desire to avoid the new classroom, I played what I knew was the winning card: I told her I didn't feel good.

"Oh honey," she exclaimed. "Let me see your throat and let's get you laying down."

There were no questions or encouragement to return to school. I was allowed to stay home for what became several weeks. Finally, at my father's behest, we visited a clinic.

I vividly remember the appointment with the no-nonsense woman doctor with short gray hair and glasses. Female physicians were rare in 1959, and she didn't waste time asking about school like the male doctors did. Following the examination, my mom and I sat across from her desk as she said, "I can't find anything wrong with her except that she's overweight. She weighs eighty-one pounds."

My mother looked at me with an expression of surprise, disappointment, and hurt as I gazed down in shame. The revelation about my weight added to my feeling of naked exposure about my imaginary malady. My plan foiled, I had no choice but to return to school.

As the sick child, I had garnered sympathy, got special food, and received precious gifts. Forced to abandon my pattern of fictitious illness that had come to dominate the household meant I lost my preferred identity.

The therapist stopped writing and looked up.

"So what was going on for you then?" she asked.

"I just wanted to be with her, to have her hold me and smile at me. If I was in bed she was paying attention to me, and I had her to myself. Everything else was too . . . scary and different." I fumbled for words.

"That's quite a story and tough to look at." She spoke with genuine empathy.

In a later therapy session I told her about the time our parents signed my sister and me up for a Christian camp in the Poconos for two weeks.

"When I was growing up, we never went to camp. Y'all are really lucky," my dad said, with a mix of pride, arrogance, and salesmanship in his southern accent.

Familiar with my father's frequent sermons on his impoverished childhood poverty, I didn't argue. But I was uncertain about this maiden trip away from my parents. I looked to my older sister, Linda, age ten, for clues on how I should respond. She yawned, intent on fastening the buttons of the burgundy cape onto her Miss America doll. I took her distraction for approval. If it was okay with her, it was okay for me.

Driving through the Poconos, we climbed narrow, serpentine roads filled with scrubby pines sweeping against a dusty blue heaven. When we arrived at the camp, we found ourselves in front of a row of brown cabins elevated from the ground on stilts with what was later going to be called distressed wood. The cabins were little more than planks nailed together to provide minimal shelter for us eager, God-fearing novices. Instead of windows, the cabin hosted black screening nailed into the frames. The wooden cross beams bore foot-high words in white paint: "Christ Died for Our Sins." I wondered if the camp counselors, whom I was yet to meet, would make me quote a Bible verse to earn passage to the toilets.

My parents helped me find my bed. It was covered with a Navy surplus blanket like the ones we had at home, common leftovers from the war. It had the hospitality of a piece of slick, gray Formica. I started crying as they began to leave.

"Hey," said my dad with enthusiasm, "you can learn to dive and show me! Linda will be here! We'll be back before you know it to visit next week." While my big sister served as a source of familiarity when she wasn't chasing or whacking me, she wasn't a source of comfort. I had no choice but to accept my fate. Mom hugged me hard as she departed, waving me away with a wistful but winning smile.

I settled in to meet my camp counselor and my cabinmates. The girl in the bed next to me was named Molly, like my younger sister. We played a game of Go Fish until suppertime, and then went to the first of many camp assemblies, punctuated by singing "This Little Light of Mine." Buoyed by the noise and vibration of one hundred singers, I did my best to be heard as we shouted, "John Jacob Jingleheimer Schmidt, YA DA DA DA DA DA DA . . ."

The camp had a circular swimming pool in addition to the lake, along with arts and crafts and, of course, Bible study. A lover of the water and desiring to please my dad, I poured myself into becoming a diving expert. Clad in our modest one-piece bathing suits, we stood in a line with eager anticipation as we moved a metal washer from the "OUT" hook to the "IN" one. This 1950s lawsuit-prevention measure was almost as much fun as the water itself.

On that first day, I eagerly followed instructions, bending down on the dock with one knee tucked under, arms out, and pushing myself into the brownish water.

The counselor was energetic. "Oh, good! You're gettin' it!" Then, "Straighten out your legs!" and "Put your head down!"

I practiced diligently as only an eight-year-old can, again and again and again, relishing the feeling of hitting the water like a floppy seal, water rushing past my ears as I stretched out my legs. However, toward the end of the week, I pushed off and went straight down into a well of frigid water. My head hit the dirt bottom of the lake hard. Crumpled and bruised, I clawed my way to the surface. In those few seconds underwater, what had been a place of play and learning turned into a lair of silent, paralyzing force. I crawled out sputtering and found the counselor. I huddled against her, soaking up her empathetic response and the support of the other campers. Scared and with the wind knocked out of me, I said a silent farewell to my diving career.

In arts and crafts, I enthusiastically made a host of key chains and wallet covers laced with plastic edging. "Indian crafts" they were called.

I became convinced that vinyl was a buffalo product. There was an added incentive to craft production, as you were recognized at the weekly Jesus jamboree for your output.

I couldn't deny that the combination of camp songs, swimming, relay races, meals, and cabin life was fun. Regardless, it took almost nothing to provoke my intense longing for home and especially the reassurance of my mother. Even looking at the lightbulbs in the cinder-blocked cafeteria set tears flying as I thought about the Sylvania 75s that lit up our modest home. I talked to Linda, who was also a bit homesick but as a ten-year-old was quieter about it. I couldn't wait for our parents' weekend visit as I feverishly earned forty Indian points for my crafts, a major achievement. I sang extra hard at the after-dinner gospel sing-alongs, masking my melancholy with sheer volume.

Finally, it was lunchtime on Sunday. In walked my dad and his mother, Mumsie, who had come to stay with us that spring. Mumsie had a smile on her face that she usually saved for salespeople or to hide her shock when people used curse words.

I ran up to my dad. "Where's Mom?" I asked.

"She's gone to visit her parents," he said lightly. "In California."

I felt like someone had put a metal ball inside my throat. I paused to take it in.

"Did she get to ride on a plane?"

"Oh, yeah," he said with enthusiasm. "Those planes are so great! She had lunch in New York and dinner in California. You know the time changes too, so she still had time to do things when she got out there. Heh, heh."

I was silent, knowing intuitively not to ask questions about when she would return. Head down, I finished my lunch, hiding the maelstrom of surprise, disappointment, and unfathomable loss. I had learned how to respond to the lies grownups told by acting as if nothing was amiss. After lunch, I walked quietly behind my father and grandmother to the pool, where my cabin competed with the other eight-year-olds in a race around the pool's perimeter.

The race I had been looking forward to became a contest of no importance. My teammate, Jane, was a somewhat heavy, slow runner. Panicked by the competition, she made a desperate attempt at speed, but didn't understand she needed to run in the shallowest part of the pool to pass the other girls. She plodded along clumsily, attempting in vain to sprint in twelve inches of water. I screamed at her sluggishness for what I saw as incompetence, pouring every bit of my own disappointment into blame for our team's loss.

I remember little of the following week except my report on arts and crafts projects. The counselor expectantly asked me how I had done this time.

"I have two pieces, but I didn't finish them," I replied softly.

"Well, we can't count them then," she said, not unkindly. I ended the week with no points at all.

When my dad and Mumsie came to pick us up the following Sunday, there was no talk of Mom's return or of my grandmother going back to her own home. I wasn't to see my mother for several months.

The therapist looked shocked. "That's terrible. How did you deal with that?" she asked.

"I focused on school and doing what my gramma told me." I then began to relate the protocols of the new regime.

Life settled in with Mumsie as the matriarch. In her earlier visits, she had allowed me to sit on her lap and push my index fingers into her deep, prune-like wrinkles. She had a nice smile most of the time and took us walking in the woods in her Girl Scout blue jean skirt, pointing out the shy jack-in-the-pulpit in the forest shade. I later learned she was a respected amateur ornithologist in the thirties who sent bird drawings to the Audubon Society that were later published.

I was, therefore, ill prepared for what awaited me when Mumsie took her place at the helm. Her demeanor resembled a no-nonsense staff sergeant with spit-shined boots and a riding crop, her chin held high. In addition, she imitated the scorched-earth policies of General Sherman's March to Atlanta charged with the responsibility of exterminating the local language and culture.

My grandmother had a particular affection for the popular Bible verse "Spare the rod, spoil the child." Mumsie was convinced that children were renegade souls whose purpose was to provide enforced scullery services in exchange for bed and board. Unquestioning obedience to the teachings of the Good Book was her credo.

Mumsie's notion of discipline did not require excellence in interpersonal relationships. Her favorite teaching story was about the one time she lied to her mother. At the age of seven she was required to perform a list of farm chores, including changing the hogs' water. The task was difficult, requiring her to climb up a fence, haul down the heavy trough, empty and refill it, and climb back up without spilling it. One day, she decided that no one would notice if she slacked off. Her mother recited the chores and inquired if she had done each one of them. When asked about the water, she responded "Yes'm," respectfully.

Unfortunately for her, her mother checked. Mumsie told us with fire in her eyes the visceral nature of a true Southern punishment with a buggy whip. The story was not for the purpose of painting her mother in an evil light. It merely illustrated the unavoidable consequences when a person—even a child—was arrogant enough to think that she was exempt from the unyielding code of obedience and honesty preached by her version of our Lord and Savior.

My younger sister has a particularly strong memory of a living room vase filled with long flexible saplings cut from a weeping willow. Known as the vase of switches, Mumsie pulled them out with particular relish when we misbehaved, waving the stinging wooden sword and punctuating her anger with a gnashing of teeth.

"You have to learn to mind!" she would rage, striking us repeatedly with amazing energy for a seventy-year-old. It was as if a demon had taken hold of her, its devilish power transmitted into the supple wood as the switches met our legs. We jumped and howled; the reddish welts festering for days.

Yet Mumsie was more than a switch-swinging enforcer, and our life continued to have activities that brought us together with laughter and belonging. She taught us how to make obscure and questionable Southern recipes such as a sweet roll dough filled with peanut butter. Full of gratitude, she hugged us with relish when we celebrated her birthday with a homemade Baked Alaska. We played board games with enthusiasm and took family drives to look at large houses with spacious lawns where rich people lived.

When we complained to our father about Mumsie, he told us she was our best friend. His answer made no sense to me, and he gave no explanation. Looking back, I feel compassion for my dad who grew up without a father himself. With a demanding job, he never imagined that he would serve as the primary caregiver of three girls. No matter how much we whined, having his mother step in and run the house was a lifesaver for him and—I can only grudgingly admit decades later—for us.

Grief has multiple faces, some resting softly, some hidden in bitterness, and others rising with a fierce pitch of anger. I hid mine by reading Superman comics, Nancy Drew mysteries, and teenage romance novels at every opportunity. The world of fantasy and adolescent attraction were far more preferable than a household of unpredictable punishments while I missed the one person I loved with true intimacy.

Like an invisible tapeworm, my mother's absence zapped my strength. Yet the sweetness of my memories remained as nourishing as a cup of cocoa on a chilly autumn day.

When we asked why Mom hadn't returned, our father explained, "The doctors say she's all mixed up and needs to be removed from her children." This was the closest he ever came to revealing a diagnosis.

He held his chin up, pointed to himself, and said, "*I'm* the sane parent."

My older sister and I looked at each other. His statement struck both of us as odd: my mother was definitely the kinder of my two parents. Neighbors loved her and held a special party for her when we moved away. My father, on the other hand, though often funny and playful, was prone to angry outbursts that frequently resulted in an old-fashioned paddling.

We lacked any information about what she was doing, and her absence puzzled us. We received only a few scattered letters over the months she was gone, with postmarks from different cities. Her mysterious absence made her feel almost unreal. Dad had first said she had gone to live with her parents in California, but he also mentioned offhandedly that she was close by. With no direct contact, we doubted we were on her mind or that she still cared about us.

Nevertheless, we got word during the holidays that year that our mother was going to take us to *The Nutcracker* in New York. We were ecstatic at not only the idea of the ballet but the idea of seeing her.

I met my mother at the bus stop in our hometown in New Jersey. Mom was dressed up with pearl earrings, a blue wool coat, and her special gray dress with fluffy snowballs at the waist. Her high cheekbones set off her curly black hair, and she looked more beautiful than any of my friends' moms. I was proud to claim her as my mother, yet I was pierced by a keen pain, knowing that she wasn't really mine anymore.

We walked into a nearby drugstore and sat down to wait for my sister, who was walking over from the neighboring school. I clung to my mother while tears streamed down my cheeks. She let it go on for a few minutes, and then moved me next to her.

"Mom, please don't go away again."

"Well," she said in a voice close to matter-of-fact, "you know you really shouldn't cry. God only gave us tears for really terrible things. And you know this isn't really terrible. Think of those little boys and girls in China who don't have any food and haven't heard about Jesus. Think about kids whose parents have died. Now those are terrible things. You really don't need to cry about this."

Reluctantly, I nodded, and my tears diminished. Linda walked in, and they hugged. We got on the bus, fighting over who would sit next to her as we chattered on about learning how to do long division. Mom told us about the ballet and the lady with the big skirt and the restaurant we were going to. We talked fast to make up for the months she had missed. What she was doing and where she lived remained unclear, like the memories I now hold of her.

The day was far beyond what we were accustomed to. We had never been to a New York City theater, as life was governed by my father's philosophy about money: It don't come back! We devoured popovers at Patricia Murphy's, taking them from a smiling lady whose only job was to make sure we had as many as we wanted. Accompanied by a woman who resembled a visiting celebrity, we saw the sugarplum dancers for the first time in a precious outing that was over too soon.

While charming and full of life that day, our mother would become a shadowy figure, appearing infrequently in our lives without explanation, always with a flash of elegance, surprise, and beauty.

As we walked to the bus to say goodbye, she talked with enthusiasm about a bell choir she was leading with young girls. I felt resentful and jealous that they got to spend time with my mom and I didn't. It was unfair that they were able to experience a closeness with her while I, her own daughter, was left out.

When I finished, the therapist paused and then said, "I understand why you stayed so long in the marriage."

I nodded and realized this was the first time anyone had voiced that thought. Someone was finally seeing why I had held onto my marriage with the determination of a puppy clinging to a special toy. Her simple acknowledgment erased my embedded shame about not having had the smarts or courage to leave before I did. It forgave me for all of those times when I had pushed down my intuition that the marriage was wrong for me. Her gentle words validated my choice of staying in a place where I was recognized and belonged, no matter how broken it was.

Chapter 10

The knotty details of a new life awaited me at home as the August days got shorter and Jenna prepared to go back to school.

John and I had a clandestine meeting in the basement to begin to hammer out the practical steps of separate lives. The fifties era windowless rec room was paneled in dark brown plywood sheets, a poor imitation of mahogany, and furnished with sagging couches and short-piled orange carpet. It felt like a dingy, neglected saloon.

"I think you should move out," I said aloud, for the first time.

"Why don't *you* move out?" he asked.

"Because I'm going to rent out a room to a female college student. They won't want to live with a man. Besides, this place is more important to me than it is to you."

He frowned. Eventually, he consented and surprised me by putting significant time into locating a new place within walking distance. As the date for our separation approached, my job prospects remained grim. My anxiety rose when I received a phone call canceling a project contract. I wondered if it had to do with my age.

As I had so many times in the past, I decided to ask him to adjust to my needs. I would ask him to stay until I had a viable work situation, I decided. He had always helped me with unforeseen expenses, seamlessly making accounts balance. Of course he would agree.

I asked him into our bedroom to talk about it. We sat on the king-size bed looking out the two windows, one of which was added during the celebrated remodel. Leaves on the maple were beginning to turn a rusty autumn red.

Years before, after the second window was installed, I had lain on the bed in awe. The tree's expansive branches, laden with deep green leaves, brought the stunning presence of Mother Earth into a room that had known so much joy and so much grim despair.

"Well, you know, I've been looking hard for a job, right?"

He nodded.

"I can't find anything I want. . . . And I'd like you to postpone the move until I do."

He let out a long sigh.

"I've spent the last two weeks looking for a place. You *knew* that."

I couldn't criticize him. He had rightfully put in extensive effort at my request, and now I wanted to render his investment useless.

"I'm scared." Familiar tears started to flow.

His expression softened. He put a hand on my shoulder and looked down. His face showed an expression of surprise approaching wonder.

"I feel liberated," he said.

It stopped me in my tracks, and yet was in a strange way affirming. The spidery web that held us together was flawed not only for me but for him. Our breakup was being validated yet also wrecking my plan to avoid the solitary existence I deeply feared and loathed.

"Please stay . . . for me. It's too much, doing all of this. Please. The house, the job, the money, being alone. Just be my safety net one more time. It's just too . . . hard."

He took me in his arms, and both of us fell back on the bed, his elbows jabbing into my upper back.

"You know," I sniffed, "I never told you enough how much I love this window and all the work you did during that project."

"I never told you how bad I felt about being so impatient and angry."

"Why couldn't we make it work?"

"It wasn't because we didn't try."

As we lay there, I poured out the unfathomable guilt I felt about the painful impact on our daughter and ending what the church called the sacrament of marriage. He gently listened, but kindly and firmly refused my request.

The children's book *The Velveteen Rabbit* describes the journey of a be-loved toy bunny. The wise skin horse tells the rabbit that toys become real because they are loved. "By that time," the skin horse says, "most of your hair has been loved off, and your eyes drop out and you get loose in the joints and very shabby."

In a strange way, I felt beautifully real and loved in that moment. My image of the impermeability of marriage was shattered; I was as ragged and frayed as the skin horse, with wounds that were raw and painful. Nevertheless, our conversation held a life-giving, open integrity. To face such sadness, look grief starkly in its face, and have it witnessed by a loved one is a rare privilege. We were confronting together the depth of what had been and the pain of its dismemberment, which is ironically one of the deepest gifts life has to offer.

Chapter 11

In the fall of 2013, I experienced my first day of feeling like I didn't have to climb out of a deep well, exhausted from the effort of walking upright. On a bright September day, four months after I'd faced the end of my marriage, I was able to engage in ordinary banter with colleagues at work, laugh about organizational gaffes, and listen to tales of summer trips to the beach. Best of all, I didn't feel the dreaded sinking feeling in my stomach, signaling an attack of panicky hopelessness. On that day, I did not imagine myself as a despondent failure. I was a competent and deserving human being with a promising future ahead.

My first halting steps felt like ascending a rickety staircase in a neglected mansion. I slowly sought to uncover a buried spirit within me that could sustain not only my return to my status as a single person but also the weight and shape of a truly innovative identity. As the days continued, I formulated a series of steadfast resolves.

First, I was determined that I would come out of this experience with a unique and better life. I was inspired by a dream I had heard about years before in which the dreamer experienced a momentous sadness. In that nocturnal fantasy, a man drove endless miles in his car over a range of steep mountains, arriving at an astonishingly beautiful oasis where he felt an overwhelming sense of peace. In his waking life soon after, his wife left him with no notice. After an agonizing period of grief, he met an extraordinary woman with whom he shared a deep and joyful bond. They became life partners. I convinced myself that this happy destiny was my fate as well, and that at some point I would trudge over the crest of a hill and find a meaningful relationship based on honoring one another's strengths.

I was committed to doing anything it took to get to a positive place emotionally and spiritually, no matter how much it cost, no matter how much trouble it took, and no matter how outlandish or weird the people who guided me were. Most important, I was willing to go as deep as I needed to, dissect my fundamental beliefs, mine what lay beneath my emotions, and release whatever held me back.

I chose to be consistently heartened by divine reminders. When anything positive or out of the ordinary occurred, I would take it as a personally designed blessing to renew my faith and cheer me forward. One day, I rode my bike to the grocery store with my keys in the black wire basket. When I got home, they were missing. I retraced all my steps only to come up blank.

Every demon took hold of me, including the notion that God was punishing me. I wrung my hands as the phone rang. It was Petco. There was a Petco tag on the key ring, and the woman triumphantly told me that the person who found them had called the pet store to get my phone number. I biked to her house, and the finder kindly produced the keys. Unfortunately, I proceeded to burden her with my entire sordid story, complete with my personal brand of tears and moans. She looked at me with wide eyes that masked the beginning of what I was sure would be a lifelong hate of Petco.

Another time I asked an auto body worker for a quote on a dented fender. He walked slowly around the car and priced the repair at $500. When I looked befittingly downcast, he gazed at me, put his hand on my shoulder, and said, "You know there are much more important things going on in this world than fixing this car. I could make it look better, but really, don't stress yourself about this."

His fatherly assessment let me dismiss the idea that I was an aging careless driver who ran into objects a bit more often than others. I didn't have to restore my vehicle nor my life to showroom perfection.

I saw both of these incidents as acts of encouragement and love from the divine. The car—and I—were okay the way we were.

As I stepped out of my fear-filled persona, I became equipped with a keen ability to sense the character and struggles of other couples. I felt as if I had exchanged a bulky overcoat for a shimmering cape through which I could feel every breeze.

One day, a friend and I sat on a picnic bench at a local park in a prosperous neighborhood. The park's shiny, new playground equipment included a massive red rubber spiderweb for climbing, child-sized houses with bright gadgets to twirl, and dozens of swings and slides set on an idyllic hill. I watched as a girl playfully pulled on the shoe of an older boy, who loudly protested as she gleefully threw it down to the woodchips below.

Across from my friend and me sat an attractive brunette woman who shouted, "Amy, now you be nice! Go pick up your brother's shoe!" She then turned to her companion, and they began to chat.

"Is she doing to do gymnastics or play volleyball?" the brunette asked her blonde friend.

"Oh, I don't know. I have to talk to Jack and see if he's willing to drive Sam to his tae kwon do lesson," she said, with a tone somewhere between playfulness and impatience.

The brunette nodded, took a sip from her water bottle, and smiled.

"At my house, I'm lobbying for a new van. Mine's had it. He wants to build a man cave in the basement for him and his buddies. Who do you think will win?" She sighed.

My friend and I continued to silently eavesdrop. In my newly single status, I found the conversation fascinating. I had participated in some version of this dialogue for more than a decade, talking to a friend about how our family would balance the precious resources of time and money as well as our own desires. I had operated with an unquestionable assumption that our family was a solid, impermeable unit, and I presumed the world believed it. I had vehemently denied the persistent, nagging feeling of a missing connection between my husband and me.

What were these two women at the playground feeling, I wondered. Was their home life as intact as their bouncy hairstyles indicated? Did their real story include an undefinable and diminishing denial and loneliness they didn't want to face? Was the actual situation as far from their cheerful sitcom banter as Donald Trump is from being a moderate?

Of course I couldn't know. Maybe they were fine. But I was burning from my fresh knowledge that outward appearances were often a lot more fragile than they appeared. I knew how easy it was to continue with safe, predictable convention rather than face a tumultuous, underlying struggle.

That afternoon in the park, my speculation about marital discord had been entirely in my head. But I soon encountered solid evidence that my intuition might have been correct.

I attended a Christmas party at a colorful Mexican restaurant. The red, green, and white Mexican flag hung over the dozens of bottles of clear tequila and amber rum. The bartender had spiked hair, enviable abs visible through his Corona T-shirt, and a smile that made me wish I was half my age. My friend and I eagerly took a seat at the bar to wait for the others, torn between acting like genteel matrons and flinging off our shirts in the hope the bartender would grab us to do the tango with a rose in his teeth.

As we chatted, an acquaintance approached and introduced herself.

I had only seen Gale from a distance. Fifteen years younger than I, she had been a model before she married, and then distinguished herself as a well-known local speaker commanding impressive fees. Her crown of curly red hair was pulled back. Her tightly fitted blouse showed a shapely bosom with a silver pendant hanging between her breasts. Even fifteen years earlier, I had never looked that good.

We chatted politely about her work and plans for the holiday season. When our group's table became available, I was surprised when she made a concerted effort to sit next to me, her body leaning forward with a focused look of attention. After we ordered, she turned squarely to me.

"I know you're divorced," she said. "Can you tell me what happened?"

"Well, lots of things I guess . . . but the biggest thing was that I felt I wanted something different."

"How old are you?" she asked.

"Sixty-three."

"Oh wow," she said, and then began to choke on her drink, her palm at her throat, doubling over. I put my hand on her back as her coughing slowed.

"Are you okay?" I asked. She nodded a bit shakily and steadied herself. I wasn't sure if she was embarrassed about being stunned by my geriatric age or just uneasy about the topic.

"So sorry about that. I'm just really surprised you left when you had an established family and you were, well, not just starting out," Gale said.

"We were in therapy for years. I couldn't live with the notion that I would rob my daughter of a family and I would lose the stability of a partner. Finally it was just vacant. There was nothing ahead for me."

She took a long swallow of her drink and was silent for a while.

"Jason and I met a long time ago, and you know. . . . It's not quite what I expected."

She paused and ordered another drink. When it arrived, she grabbed it like a life raft.

"We met when I was younger, and he was the CEO of the company. Then I started my career, and it's really different now." Her voice faded, and I felt a genuine sense of empathy for her.

She wasn't the only woman who took me aside and grilled me: *How did you do it?* Several asked. How could you possibly leave a marriage in later life with decades of memories and serious financial consequences? Some were even angry or at least confused, it seemed, that I had chosen to leave a relationship that was supportive in so many ways. They then laid out the emptiness they were experiencing in what appeared to others as happy, functioning homes. All I could do was nod, trying not to judge them or congratulate myself for my courage, smugly asserting that I had all the answers. I knew exactly how hard it was to sit where they were sitting, unwilling to face a desert of feelings and the life-changing implications for acknowledging them.

Crawling out of my personally designed airtight bimbo of matrimonial happiness, I came to see the end of my marriage as completely disconnected from failure. Eliminating my self-imposed judgment—not only for committed partnerships but for other life ventures—ultimately offered me the deepest solace and greatest freedom.

The divorce forced me to deal with endings, the very things I had avoided with such determination for so many years. As time passed, I began to see that there was no dishonor or harm in ending a commitment that was no longer alive and vital. I began the slow process of accepting the completion of my marriage as I focused on forces that encouraged the unflinching forces of life.

My solid sense of faith in a divine energy was my greatest ally. The wisest and most consistent teacher was the earth itself. When fall, my favorite season, ends, I am sad but don't become resentful when the brilliant autumn leaves drift to the ground and crumble into crisp brownish dust. Likewise, as the cherry trees drop their last sumptuous berries in my backyard, I don't blame them for going to sleep until the tiny white flowers burst forth the following May and spawn a new crop of fruit. Even with the onslaught of winter, I may complain a bit, but I accept the oncoming cold as a part of life, confident that the warmer cycle will return and the sun's comforting rays will produce another harvest in its own time.

I remembered the trident-bearing Hindu god Shiva I had mused about earlier in the therapist's office. While his sister deity Kali is a bearer of darkness, Shiva is a positive entity. Sometimes called the destroyer, he annihilates things that interfere with supporting and perpetuating life for the future of the world. His demolition eases the flow of events from one level to another, hastening the destruction of forms that no longer serve—a sort of cosmic recycling agent. Imagining that I wore his tattoo on my forehead, I could even muster a measure of pride and adopt him as my mentor.

With these cosmic teachers and the presence of a gentle grace, I decided that I would really rather keep my arm, not whack it off as I had been willing to do earlier in order to keep my marriage intact. The season of my life had changed, and I was able to say the word "divorce." Slowly I began to see that this ending offered an outstretched hand of vitality and newness built on the successes and lessons of the past, instead of a searing failure for which I could not forgive myself.

I had the privilege of knowing many people who kept reminding me of that. Even though the marriage was over, the love we shared was still there. We had held and supported each other in everything from the deaths of both of our fathers to the extraordinary joy of adopting a child. A vital bond remained even though our partnership had dissolved. Yes, criticism, disrespect, and anger had also been present, but these human emotions did not diminish our capacity to build our lives with strength and sensitivity, passing on our hard-earned wisdom to those we loved now and would love in the future.

My loss taught me to see an ending as a time of permission to let go. That is the normal course of life. When I made the mistake of explaining this concept to some individuals, their eyes expanded to the size of a famished blowfish and then politely gazed downward. Some people with highly progressive ideas in many areas are immovable when I mention the need to dismantle the matrimonial bond. They believed that marriage is supposed to be lifelong, with no exceptions allowed for change or growth. Or perhaps their discomfort was due to their own battles and captivity to worn-out beliefs. I came to know deeply that we face the frightening disintegration of what we count on in our own time and in our own way. In doing so, I was freed from the bondage of lifeless agreements, and I could reclaim the energy and vitality of creating something that was truly my own.

Chapter 12

In September 2013, our marriage had been over for four months. Our decision was not yet public, and we continued to live together, disconsolately sorting out our now separate futures. While I had ignored the implications of losing my daughter half time, I had thought obsessively about the reality of being without a built-in plus one for social events. I now had the identity I despised: a single mom. I decided to step out and make a clandestine debut of my new status. Rowan, my funniest friend, kindly picked me up in her black Prius. My husband stood in the front yard as we departed, waving a sorrowful goodbye.

Rowan and I drove to a farm in Wisconsin to eat homegrown beets, bib lettuce, and a poor baby steer named Hector. We sat around a hand-hewn oak table with solid legs stained the color of a rich tea. The accompanying benches were as firm and stable as the earth beneath them.

A craft table was set up with linoleum tiles and a simple press, allowing the kids to capture impressions of the brilliant foliage with dazzling tubes of orange and crimson ink. The long-haired art teacher assisted the youngsters in creating their own souvenirs. A grinning five-year-old with curly, raven hair and two front teeth missing held her masterpiece high.

"Look, Daddy!" she chattered with delight, as her father smiled gently.

"Wow!" he said, with a smile. "Let's put that right on the refrigerator with those magnets you like."

My new status—although unknown to others—put a muzzle on my limited repartee. With a twisted smile, I awkwardly conversed with other parents as we stood next to the white clapboard porch. Madge, a bleach blonde with round, oversized spectacles and an athletic build, confidently described her son's success with the hockey team.

"I just know they'll take state this year, don't you think?"

Hassan, another parent, said, "Well, that's good. What are you doing about how much time they spend on computers? Is that good for them? She doesn't really answer my questions anymore, you know."

Madge answered with a smirk, "Just take away their phones. That's where you get some action."

I felt envious about the ease with which they discussed their family lives as the farm host approached. He was a scrappy, bearded man with shoulder length hair and faded bib overalls. Speaking in a muffled tone, he walked us through the rows of the almost ready-to-pick autumn harvest.

I had never seen broccoli in its original growing form. The plant resembled a small tree with the main stalk standing almost three feet high. Broad, leathery leaves poked out of the trunk surrounding small groups of florets every few inches. It looked like a series of broccoli villages sitting comfortably on a vertical hill. They provoked a tiny bit of welcome in this angst-filled evening.

As we sat down to eat, I looked anxiously for Rowan, not wanting to sit by myself. She saw my look and came over, sharing a kind, private smile as she eased onto the seat next to me. The small children swung their feet on the high benches. An air of community hung over the table buoyed by a dusty blue sky and a rusty setting sun. Adults passed heavy platters of yellow squash, large bowls of salad heaped with purple heirloom tomatoes, and slabs of poor Hector who had been a treasured pet the week before. Plates were filled, and even the children welcomed vegetables with their bright, fresh colors, making them look like festive treats. Witnessing the miracle of food grown on that very land created an atmosphere of nourishment, as if the earth was engulfing us with laughter and gratitude.

I remembered another meal. On a trip to Mexico more than twenty years earlier, John and I took a day trip to see some ancient pictographs. The van, filled with other tourists, stopped for a picnic lunch at a primitive outdoor site. There were no tables or chairs, only some large rocks beside a narrow stream. The staff set the lunch boxes down on the ground.

I picked up my meal and settled down on a stone near the other guests. There was nowhere else to sit, so John came over and stood next to me, calmly eating his pimento-flecked penne pasta salad and an oversized chocolate chip cookie. He stood there quietly and chewed slowly, unconcerned in the noonday shade. It was such a small thing, having him occupy a place close to me where I could feel his warmth and affection, projecting a sense of stability as firm as a grandmother oak. Now that was gone, and I acutely felt its absence.

I loved being married. I loved its safety, affection, meals, laughter, protection, events with other families, and his unquestionable presence at my side. Although I didn't want to admit it, I also coveted the automatic acceptance and higher status that came along with marriage in the socially conservative Midwest. It had added an unacknowledged yet surprising confidence to my identity.

Marriage had become my skin, an integral, embedded part of myself. Now the membrane was sloughing off, like a snake shedding its skin. Unlike the slithery reptile, I found its disappearance terrifying. I clung to my married self, convinced its loss would cause me to disappear.

And so, skinless with a crooked grin, I survived the first foray into singlehood buoyed by my friend Rowan, a kind substitute on that sweet autumn night. On the ride home she asked, "Are you okay?"

"Of course I am. Well, at least I am better off than good old Hector smothered in barbeque sauce."

We snorted with giggles. Too soon, she dropped me at home to continue to weave the next chapter of who I was to become.

Chapter 13

John moved out on a Saturday in October amidst a rusty fan of autumn color. He took a small but precious number of items with him. I had forgotten that the handsome, ingeniously designed sewing cabinet and the matching blond coffee table had been handcrafted by his father. I had come to think of them as my own. They reminded me of Art's hearty and sometimes bawdy laugh, along with his captivating stories of Finnish mail-order brides in northern Minnesota in the early twentieth century.

I spent moving day at a meditation retreat cowering in an uncomfortable wooden auditorium chair that reminded me of elementary school assemblies. I shifted my position as frequently as a cat swatting a pesky fly, obediently muttering the promises of loving kindness even though they seemed distant and unattainable: *May you be happy, may you be free, may you live a life of ease.*

The following day, a friend dropped by. She stood in the small aqua-colored entryway gazing at the lemon-colored wall in the living room that now hosted only a solitary picture hook. The vacant sixty-year-old plaster seemed embarrassed by the departure of the one-of-a-kind cabinet. To the right sat a bare section of oak floor containing two rubber brown furniture floor protectors. They were the only remnants of a favorite olive-green easy chair where I had nestled with our cats Charlie and Lissa for years. The flowered pillows on the couch were askew, and the only remaining rocking chair sat awkwardly alone next to the bay window.

My friend gazed at the haphazard display that was now my living room. Without knowing what had occurred, her first words were, "It smells like someone died here." The house was in a state of mourning: my former sanctuary seemed to weep for its missing members and a life it no longer had.

When she left, I went to the pantry and pulled out the middle shelf of the custom-made cabinets that still slid soundlessly as if oiled with butter. I filled my hands with caramelized peanuts. I could count on these dependable companions to dull any concern. As I stood munching, I reminded myself that we had been living separate lives for years. What was I missing anyway? Weren't the current circumstances cause for celebration, I mused, as another handful of nuts made its tasteless journey down my throat.

The next day I returned from an evening out with friends. The steps and side door were shrouded in a sinister darkness. Only weeks before, I was welcomed by a shimmering pool of light around the entryway. John thoughtfully turned the light on every time I returned after dark. On those many nights, it was as if the dainty brilliance said, "Hey ya—come on in, sweetheart, and rest yourself." I was particularly touched because his memory wasn't the greatest. The kindly gesture gave me a sense of cozy belonging, like a baby owl coming back to the nest after its first flight.

On this night, a few days into living alone, I stumbled clumsily up the cement, felt for the lock, and was relieved as the key entered and turned. I walked into a hollow darkness and silence as I fumbled for the light switch. No one was staying up for me, I noted bitterly, as I shuffled through the vacuous building, my feet touching the floorboards I had chosen so carefully and full of hope eight years before.

The next morning, I looked out the bedroom window as I was dressing and saw a pair of squirrels in a dizzying chase around the maple tree. Mesmerized by their energy, I continued to gaze at them as my right hand reached for my bra in the nearby dresser drawer. Instead of touching a soft pile of slippery nylon, my fingers tapped the naked grain of the wood in an empty drawer. With my ex-husband—aka laundress—absent, my soiled garments were sitting on the cold cement basement floor waiting for attention.

For years I had thoughtlessly shoved my clothes down the bathroom laundry chute. They would magically appear on my bed, socks in neat little uterus-shaped nests and tiger undies paired with the old lady nylon ones that went up to my waist. I snatched them up absentmindedly when I was late for an appointment, without a shred of gratitude for my spouse, who loaded the soiled blue linens, jeans, and tops into the washer without complaint week after week. Grudgingly, I realized I would have to relearn this unwanted skill.

I recalled one day years earlier when I slept in under the cozy bamboo sheets. With a bearlike stretch, I noted the brilliant green of the spring maple tree. I suddenly saw the time and raced downstairs, hurriedly eating a piece of half-burned toast as John returned from taking our daughter to school. He stopped and sighed.

"You know the credit card balance was $500 more than you said it was going to be."

I continued my accelerated chewing.

"Well, the flights went up for our trip to see my sisters," I said, as an airborne bite of toast hit the cat in the head, sending him fleeing downstairs.

I shrugged, wiped my face with a dish towel, and looked for my purse.

"I have a coffee date," I said, as I made one last dry swallow, "just transfer some money," and walked out the door.

I heard no more about it. Like many things that happened in my marriage, I was protected from the consequences of my actions and allowed to operate with the recklessness of a teenager.

I normally think of containers as those handy plastic objects full of olive oil–soaked grape leaves that I stuff my fingers in when no one is looking. In the case of my divorce, however, containers were the welcome patterns that sustained me. They were a daily familiar, as one teacher called them, and they didn't have to be uniformly positive. Counting on him to mitigate financial hiccups and create an endless supply of neat undergarments manifested predictability, caring, and the integrity of my home.

It was this lack of ordinariness, or what some call the ADLs—activities of daily living—that were the hardest for me to bear in those early days. Our separation put a spotlight on the countless gestures and repeated, unconscious behaviors that supported me. They had solidified themselves into my ordinary rhythm, so much a part of my being that I didn't notice them. I was now acutely aware of their absence.

During those first few months after the divorce, my spouse and I, in our parental wisdom, decided our daughter would go back and forth each week between the two residences. One Sunday evening, a month into the new schedule, it was time for Jenna to go to her dad's. I walked into her room and found her sound asleep, exhausted from an afternoon of Ultimate Frisbee practice and writing a paper on the Black Panthers. She was huddled under the giant orange-and-blue-flowered comforter she had excitedly chosen in middle school. Her stark black hair spread over the duvet like an ebony fan, hiding a body that was almost full-grown but still a child's in so many ways. A small straw suitcase sat at the foot of her bed.

I felt the same tenderness I had when I held her hand and walked her to school when she barely came up to my waist. To wrest her from this peaceful state and displace her from the sanctuary we had so carefully built felt like a sin. Nevertheless, I obeyed my resolve to act as a grown-up, fairly adhering to our agreement, with an unspoken promise to keep my own emotions to myself. I leaned over as gently as possible and touched her shoulder.

"Jenna, wake up. It's time to go," I said, ignoring her cries of "I'm tired." Although she was sixteen and driving, I could see only a tiny child as she sleepily put on a hoodie and jeans. I carried the tiny suitcase into the car, marking the end of our time together and the beginning of a week of solitude.

To assuage my own guilt, discomfort, and denial, I did everything possible to ease the transition into a bifurcated household. I picked up a Raggedy Ann scarecrow to put on the porch of John's rental duplex along with some baby pie pumpkins for Halloween. Jenna and I picked out a new set of sheets with toy trains (her choice). I knew John's notion of gourmet meals was raw celery and forks full of braunschweiger. To thwart his culinary ignorance, I dropped off hot dish casseroles topped with bacon bits and sour cream.

These acts created, I thought, an energetic connection between us and allowed me to maintain a sense of family. However, my daughter saw them differently and scornfully rebuked me for my deliveries.

"You don't know how to be divorced!"

Responding to her angry words, I faced her squarely and confessed, "You're right, I don't. I've never done it before."

Although I thought my comeback would gain me points, it served only to elicit a look of unveiled disdain.

As autumn drifted into winter, I sent out a plea to family members about coming for Christmas. I couldn't bear not having days of laughter, inappropriate jokes, and a kind familiarity that had become my idea of a holiday. I was elated when both sisters, a niece, and my stepmother agreed. We managed to do a Minnesota version of the holiday, complete with church, brunch, and games. We played a word game with my daughter's friend, whose first language was not English. He got the winning score by spelling the word "genitals."

As we giggled with raucous laughter, I silently observed that mentioning one's private parts would never have happened if we had gathered when I was still a wife. If my marriage hadn't ended and John hadn't moved out, my extended family wouldn't have been in my beautiful home, and we wouldn't be having a fairly amazing new kind of holiday. I also knew that the sweetness of their presence was because my heart was broken, and each peal of laughter was helping to gently mend it.

PART II

Chapter 14

It was my first winter as a single mom. Jenna's school was hosting a fund-raiser at a venue that didn't have basketball hoops or gum stuck under the tables. It had an actual cloak room, drinks with alcohol and ice, and cuisine that did not include undercooked spaghetti and RAGÚ tomato sauce. As I entered the venue from the frigid air, my quilted maroon coat and furry Mukluk boots made me look like a puffy scarecrow who had been swallowed by bears. I wore my only evening dress that fit and had been purchased less than ten years ago. Looking in the mirror in the restroom, I rummaged around for a tube of Mary Kay lipstick from the nineties, pursed my lips, and entered the gala room.

My friend Amy, another divorcee, agreed to be my date. We took in the tea lights and tinsel streamers while looking for a bargain among the silent auction contributions of baskets of preschool books, wine bottles, and miscellaneous jewelry. A parent who had not been written up in *Rolling Stone* strummed a bass as another half-heartedly brushed the drums. With relief, I found a teacher who knew our family and its current status.

"Great to see you! This is my first time out to an event this winter, and it's kind of rough."

She said nothing, but beamed and waved at the woman behind me.

"Your daughter's doing great," she said to me, as she hugged my arm and got up to speak to another parent behind me.

Deflated, I found my friend and ran into another guest I knew well enough to tell her the news of my single status.

She leaned over and said, "Good for you! No one I know is happy."

I was surprised by her candidness and affirmation. She offered no details but waxed on about the entertaining details of her life on an adult mental health unit, which served as welcome comic relief to parenting six kids.

"One of them tried to lock herself in the other day and then threw up on the EKG machine, but I outsmarted her with an extra key." She grinned.

I laughed at her unflagging humor and grit. The auctioneer began, encouraging us to hold up our cardboard donation card to fund new tents and sleeping pads for a summer camping trip. The enthusiastic leader then asked for donations of $5,000, working down in $100 increments. My friend and I felt increasingly cheap, poor, and mortified, finally raising our hands for a $25 gift. By this time, the crowd was pleasantly tipsy. They shouted good-naturedly while a low hum of laughter droned on in the back of the room. The bidding concluded, and cheerful parents and staff began to disband.

Amy had departed earlier so I was left to navigate the coatroom on my own. Couples pressed against one another while recovering their heavy wraps. I awkwardly sat on the radiator and donned my boots, buttoning and gloving up in preparation for the outside chill of ten degrees.

I stepped outdoors into the frigid evening. In spite of the night's untroubled and quiet darkness, I walked the block to my car with a feeling of restlessness and lack. It was, I realized, the first time I had had to make my way home after an evening event without John. He always strode silently but firmly next to me, touching my arm and making sure I didn't fall on the ice, or else he went for the car and let me stand in the foyer savoring the warmth. A walk to the car: it was so ordinary, such a nothing, except that it evoked a giant something, a priceless gesture of connection and belonging.

Reaching the car, I sat down on the hard, cold driver's seat and turned on the radio to a crooning voice from a local radio station. It was a jazzy number, the drummer skillfully brushing the cymbals as the singer's voice rose and fell. The car slowly heated up, making it an agreeable shelter as I drove along the empty streets.

As I pulled into my driveway, I noticed the full moon over the roof of my darkened house, surrounded by what looked like an icy halo. Very faintly, a group of stars twinkled shyly in the inky night, their blinking lights determined to shine.

Chapter 15

In the early days of my marriage, I had a conversation with my boss, one of a handful of women who had risen to leadership in the organization. An independent spirit, she had never married, and possessed an uncanny political savvy that allowed her to hire people—including me—during hiring freezes. With her boisterous voice, you could hear her coming halfway down the hall. I casually mentioned that my tires were dangerously low.

"You didn't check them?" she asked.

"No," I said dismissively, "he does it."

She looked at me inquisitively but said nothing, then turned away to speak to a waiting employee.

In earlier days when I shared a car with roommates, I had cheerfully run the gas gauge down to the red line. The next person driving found herself stranded far from a gas station with no help in sight and a particularly colorful vocabulary for me. I felt my own responsibilities were too important to bother with such trifles.

In the fall of 2014, a year after our separation, I was driving home at night on a fairly deserted road that was in the process of being regraded. The asphalt looked like bolts of corduroy with neat, engraved lines running horizontally down its path. The manholes were substantially higher than usual, making the avenue resemble an oversized prairie dog village that had accidentally come to the wrong neighborhood.

I am usually dismissive not only toward cars but also toward the physical universe in general. I have frequently stopped in the middle of airplane aisles when people are behind me, creating a scene resembling lab rats panting over a pile of pellets, annoying the passengers, and arousing the ire of my daughter. Blithely ignorant on that autumn night, I gave no thought to the other cars gingerly creeping down the road at twenty miles per hour—until I passed them all and smacked into a protruding manhole. I heard a loud, unwelcome crash.

I pulled over and got out. The tire wasn't just flat; it was shredded, bringing to mind a birthday cake ravaged by two-year-olds. I sighed and called AAA. I then immediately called my ex, an action as habitual and instinctive as turning on the hot water while preparing for a bath.

It was a balmy fall evening, the moon peeking over a dusty charcoal sky. I was across the street from the now abandoned train depot and in front of a building with no sign. I determined that I was in no immediate physical danger, but the absence of people caused me to be keenly alert.

My ex arrived and reminded me with a sullen face and hands on his hips that this was the third tire I had destroyed in six months. He then proceeded to ask a litany of questions. Yes, I'd called AAA. Yes, I'd been going too fast. Yes, I had a spare. He continued his investigation, kneeling to examine the car's carriage as I accepted his testy scowl and poorly cloaked resentment about having been summoned. I was glad there weren't any lights available to shine into my eyes.

Meanwhile, a car came out of the parking lot wearing that ever dependable shield: *to serve and protect.* My car had broken down in front of a police station.

As a white woman with gray hair, I don't carry the scars of a fearful and violent history with law enforcement. When the officer opened a window, I was confronted by a policeman who grumpily asked me what I was doing there, no happier with my presence than my ex. When I pointed to my disabled vehicle, he closed his window in disgust. An hour passed, and other cars came and went, one containing a woman officer who was genuinely concerned. My ex, though lacking a laser pointer, continued his presentation on automobile care.

"Well," he said, kneeling down and pointing the flashlight under the car. "You can see how low it is. There wasn't much clearance." He looked at me accusingly as his tone asked: *What were you thinking?*

I attempted an innocent lopsided smile.

We continued to wait restlessly as AAA sorted out our location. Unrelenting, my ex waxed on about the importance of oil changes, power train warranties, and the Darth Vader nature of road obstacles. Somewhere in the middle of that time, I heard a voice of cosmic clarity.

Katherine, your car broke down in front of a police station on a beautiful night. You couldn't be safer. You called the needed resource and did everything right.

And then, pointedly, *You don't need him!*

I looked up, blocking out the human car care manual. I saw the shiny moon and listened to the silence of a magical, shimmering evening. Life was taking care of me in the kindest way. It didn't matter that I didn't want to be independent and had, out of habit, reached for an unnecessary and crabby liberator. The situation was demonstrating not only my common sense and capabilities, but the humorous, goofy, luminous hammock of the divine, which catches us when we are unsure of ourselves, panicked, and don't think we can possibly cope. It was also telling me that there was no way I could grow, mature, and thrive when I continued to rely on an outgrown relationship. The assumptions I had about a need for a care-taker/adult babysitter/mechanic/laundress were false. I would be taken care of, even when I made careless or reckless choices.

Buoying up my own capabilities was a powerful force holding me as steadily and fiercely as Mary held Jesus in swaddling clothes. My dependence on the rescuer shrank a bit on that sweet September evening, and an acorn of confidence began to grow. Something way larger than AAA had my back. Its only premium was my willingness to accept its bounty, step out of a shadow of unnecessary protection, and accept my innate ability to wield my courage, strength, and wisdom.

Chapter 16

The American Midwest is generally known for its boredom, flatness, family values, and avoidance of anything remotely newsworthy. Even so, I tend to agree with Walt Whitman, who proclaimed in his book *Specimen Days*, "I am not so sure but the prairies and plains, while less stunning at first sight [than Yosemite, Niagara Falls, the Upper Yellowstone], last longer, fill the esthetic sense fuller, precede all the rest, and make North America's characteristic landscape."

As a lifelong seeker, I jump at opportunities to experience the hidden face of the spirit in physical form. In the fall of 2016 I was offered the chance to participate in a vision quest in Bear Butte, South Dakota, the site where the celebrated Lakota warrior Crazy Horse offered prayers for his people.

The vision quest tradition is practiced in a variety of forms. Participants typically don't eat or drink for the length of the quest, which is usually several days. The seeker is confined to a small, contained area, such as a twenty-foot square, to enable a strong sense of focus and reflect on one's life journey and purpose. The sparse equipment may include a sleeping bag and perhaps a tent. There is often no writing and absolutely no phones—just oneself to deal with—along with the life force and mystery of the earth itself.

The invitation came from an Anishinaabe elder, lending an aura of respect, honor, and authority to the pursuit. The accompanying guide, also an elder, generously drove an hour to talk to me about the details of the undertaking and calm any fears I had.

A requirement of this passage was the making of prayer ties. In a state of meditation and prayer, the seeker takes a small, square, three-inch piece of cloth and inserts a pinch of tobacco. The small bundle is then tied carefully with a piece of yarn or string. The completed tie represents prayers, intentions, and good wishes.

For this particular quest, I was expected to bring not a single prayer tie, but four hundred of them, divided into lots of one hundred dressed in the four sacred colors of a traditional medicine wheel: white, black, red, and yellow. In addition, I had to create four larger prayer ties roughly the size of tennis balls in the same four colors.

I gulped but resolved to do it. I would let the tying of each bundle represent the desire of my heart to let go of the life I had been leading and make space for beginning anew.

While the prospect of making so many bundles was demanding, being on a mountain with minimal shade, alone, in September carried its own trepidation. I imagined my parched, dehydrated body on a treeless, arid surface, facing my demons—to say nothing of snakes and hungry mosquitoes—in misery. The sun is strong and unforgiving in those days before the fall equinox, and the evenings host a chill. I couldn't predict the steepness of the mountain, and the thought of ascending it with a tent, sleeping bags, and my personal gear was daunting. I had already asked and been granted permission to have water, due to my intermittent heart issue; but, I realized, I would still have to carry the additional burden of heavy gallon jugs up to the site.

An increasingly compelling internal voice insisted that I needed to take this step to root out the demons that had placed a stake in my body and psyche. I prepared with the firm belief that this unnerving task would provide much needed solace and healing, dispelling my frequent attacks of darkness. It was these pesky forces, I believed, that had kept me trapped in an old identity that I neither needed nor wanted. I still felt like I was stuck in a dress with a broken zipper, flailing my arms and unable to extricate myself. This undertaking, I imagined, would illuminate why I was unable to hold firmly onto a sense of confidence, command, and well-being. Nevertheless, the journey felt incredibly hard at a time when the most persistent advice I received from many was: "Be kind to yourself." Although I smiled and said thank you, I was clueless about what it meant.

As the departure date drew closer, my pile of prayer ties grew higher, filling a large straw basket. I enjoyed the reflective time the task provided as I sat on my house porch in the late summer, watching teenagers run by, children biking with determination, and couples holding hands. Unfortunately, my anxiety mounted at the same speed as the youthful bikers when I thought about a solitary time outdoors, without the most basic comforts and facing the nasty landscape of my tattered soul.

Each day the voice felt harsher, as if a judgmental deity had condemned me to this perilous venture. Then I got a surprise, unsolicited phone call from the Anishinaabe elder. Although we had never met, he offered a special carrying stick to transport my prayer ties up the mountain. His kind words brought me to tears. Surely, as these unknown beings had decided to care for me, I had an obligation to proceed. Wasn't that the best way to honor my path?

A few days before leaving for Bear Butte, I felt like I was preparing for a perilous, maiden flight to the nearest asteroid with an untested spacesuit. I wanted to get out of it desperately, yet I feared I would be abandoning a critical passageway if I did so, rejecting the kindness of the many people who had reached out to me.

Finally, I phoned a teacher whom I had worked with and described my plight. She laughed in a gentle way.

"No, Katherine," she said and sighed. "What you are thinking is the old way. You think it is your lot to suffer. That way is always hard. That's the way you've gone all of your life. For you, the hard way is familiar. There are always a thousand ways to move forward, and this isn't yours right now. Just let it go."

I couldn't describe my relief. I thanked her profusely and only regretted that I needed permission from someone else to tell me that hardship was unnecessary and that a far less rigorous approach was not only possible but preferable.

Ecstatic with my reprieve, I felt an exuberant, unaccustomed freedom to plan my own pilgrimage. I took my battered 2008 Honda and equipped it for travel with Jane Austen's *Emma* on a CD, a cooler full of organic carrots, boxes of energy bars, a sleeping bag and mat, and a borrowed tent.

My first major stop was Pipestone National Monument. It is the only place in the world where pipestone is mined by hand solely by Native people. As its name suggests, the stone is used for pipes in ceremonial gatherings and for personal use by those called to pray in that way. I heard the light tap of hammers as I walked slowly along the dirt paths accompanied by a faint chink, chink, chink sound. The carvers were invisible to me, hidden in wide crevices behind the rich foliage as they harvested bits of the sacred stone. I was stunned by the quietness of the land, the ocher hue of the pipestone, and the sense of deep peace.

I stopped at places of such import as the Corn Palace (really a large gym) in Mitchell, South Dakota, and Wall Drug (a not-so-fancy Walmart) on my way to the Badlands. I was drawn to the Badlands by their moonlike landscape set on the flatness of South Dakota's great plains. The mysterious rusty, layered landforms appeared suddenly and majestically, peeking above the billboards like giant mushrooms, causing my excitement to mount.

I drove to the Badlands National Park entrance and was directed to my campsite, a barren piece of grass lacking anything redeeming. The stunning land formations were far away and only faintly visible. The other campers, couples of course, looked at me with as much interest as a sated koala bear after devouring a batch of eucalyptus leaves. It was 3:00 p.m., the hour when, unbeknownst to me, the winds kick up with swiftness and force. I pulled out the worn, borrowed tent, assembled the poles, and proceeded to anchor the center one in the dirt. I then began to attach the nylon tent to it, which immediately flew up like a skirt on a blustery day. I grabbed one end as the entrance flap shot out of reach in the opposite direction. The other campers continued their leisurely dedication to their cans of Coors, oblivious to my fate. I looked in vain at the empty horizon, hoping for a rescue party.

Resting for a moment, I tried it again, grasping the center pole firmly with one hand, while attempting to attach the cleat to the pole with the other. I then heard a brisk snapping sound. The center anchor pole had broken cleanly in two. With the main lynchpin severed, the tent flailed in the breeze like a debutante's gown. My shelter was now officially disabled. Relieved in a strange way, I walked to the nearby lodge and asked about a room. Full, I was told.

I wandered over to a picnic table, a lackluster metal structure where countless families had enjoyed the sweeping expanse. I sat down with the knowledge that my plans were dashed, as was my budget. I rested quietly for a time, and then turned my head and saw the manifestation of God in South Dakota: a billboard that said in three-foot letters: "KOA— 3 Miles Away."

I had happened on the heart of cheap lodging and American confidence! I dialed the number and was told the camper cabins were full, but they had a teepee open, with bedding. O blithe spirit of renewal, recovery, and faith! I was sure the three wise men weren't happier when they finally spied the mythical stable of our Lord! Who would have thought KOA possessed such a friendly connection with divine intervention?

Elated, I eagerly drove the three miles. Unlike the bare park campground, the KOA site was lined with homey cottonwood trees bordering a small humming creek. I drove to my teepee, a good-sized one, and pulled in. The mesmerizing shapes of the Badlands were actually larger, closer, and far more scenic than at the park site. The location also had an air of serenity without the institutional feel of a government-owned campground. I could not believe my luck.

I nestled into my teepee on a frayed foam rubber mattress that KOA supplied. I then ventured outside to munch on a hearty turkey salad from my cooler and watch the sun go down. The streaks of rose and orange were like smears from a celestial palette hovering over the sandy-colored mounds. The departing sun cast a gentle shadow on the beech leaves and meandering creek. After walking the property perimeter as a way to mark the tremendous fortune of the day, I sat down on a rock outside the teepee next to a fire ring.

I gathered a bundle of sticks and set them into the pit. Using pine cones and stray pieces of birch bark, I started a modest fire. I then took my basket of four hundred prayer ties and methodically burned them while the smoke curled into the sky.

I watched soberly, considering the tradition I was honoring and the ancestors who seemed to be patiently watching me from behind the grove of oaks. I took in the blessed moisture of the singing water, watching my abundant prayers make their way slowly into the vault of blue, knowing they were heard in a way I couldn't understand. At peace with my unlikely progress, I retired into my modest abode.

⚜ ⚜ ⚜

The Lakota people were the first ones to call the Badlands "mako sica" or "land bad," due to sweltering temperatures, sparse water, and a treacherous landscape. Visitors were bitten by snakes and sizzled raw by the sun. Its small hills are more reminiscent of a mesmerizing *Star Wars* panorama than our home planet. The dunes have a sandy texture and slant upward like human-sized anthills. There are few trees, making the dazzling colors of the rock keenly visible. Their dome-like shapes display rainbow hues of grayish clays, earthy browns, and vibrant, rusty oranges. Humans now walk here easily, thanks to the national park trail system, which offers a unique experience of mystery on the earth's multicolored crust.

I had planned to stay there three nights. The first day, I enthusiastically started out on a seven-mile hike. The path was marked by sticks about five feet high, their tips dipped in red paint. While the crimson landmarks were supposed to make the signposts visible, they were frightfully easy to lose track of in the high grasses and numerous rolling hills. After less than half a mile, I became disoriented from my path three times. I was distressed enough to record a video, which I sent to my family telling them where I was if I went missing. Soon I agreed with the original Lakota residents and packed up, heading to my final destination.

Bear Butte is six miles outside of Sturgis, South Dakota. I decided I would do a reconnaissance mission to prepare for my ascent the next day. Embarrassed about encountering the people who had invited me on their quest, I sunk low into the driver's seat and donned a large pair of fuchsia sunglasses, hoping to be mistaken for Meryl Streep. I need not have worried. The area is expansive and has numerous visitors. I entered the empty parking lot in the late afternoon to assess the butte's difficulty and estimate how long it would take to climb with my less than Olympic capacity. The park was quiet, surrounded by flatlands for miles, and featured an easy, well-maintained trailhead entrance. My fears calmed, I set off to the hotel.

Deadwood, South Dakota, is a combination of Cody, Wyoming, and Atlantic City. The town is full of casinos, flashing lights, and embellished store signs of mythical heroes. A rustic wooden sign marks the location of Wild Bill Hickok's demise. I saw a respectable amount of foot traffic, bustling restaurants, and even an actual traffic jam. A portrait of Wyatt Earp invited visitors to keno games. I wistfully passed them as I headed to my bargain hotel on the west side of town, which sported the charm of a soon-to-be-abandoned Kmart.

Settled into my hotel room, I felt both relief and expectancy about my much-anticipated climb. I sat down on the bed to eat my takeout salad and turned on the television. I realized with delight that the final movie in *The Lord of the Rings* trilogy, *The Return of the King*, was on. Frodo, the hero, and Sam, his loyal sidekick, journey to the fiery Mordor volcano to destroy the cursed ring that was causing the spread of evil in the world. Frodo, the hero, is appallingly weak as well as crazed with the evil spell of the ring. His eyes gleam with a deranged wickedness, and he's so debilitated he can't make it up the final ascent. Sam has to pick up the bewitched Frodo and carry him on his back to the final cliff. Even as Frodo has given up, Sam's quiet, consistent support gives him the energy and literally an extra set of legs to fulfill his sacred mission, destiny, and commitment: destroying the ring and returning the world to balance.

In his delirium, Frodo dons the malevolent ring, making him invisible. He and Gollum battle for the prize on the cliff's precarious edge. Locked together in lethal combat, they tumble over the precipice. Gollum falls to his death as Frodo catches the rocky ledge. Sam then reaches down, pulling Frodo to safety.

I watched the film spellbound, my wilted lettuce sitting idly on my plastic fork. It was my story on the screen. I knew, as was true for everything that had happened to me in that hair-raising time, it was no accident that a TV station in South Dakota was showing this timeless tale. I was being reminded that I could not have come here on my own. The invitation of a generous elder whom I had never met had put me in exactly the right place. I wasn't Crazy Horse and didn't need to imitate him or unthinkingly accept a path designed by others, even though they were revered and extraordinary. I needed instead to create my own way of surrendering the toxicity and attachment to my own past, designing my own passageway to freedom; and, I thought with a tiny bit of glee, I had done just that.

I reached the butte about 9:00 a.m. the following day. Only one other car was in the parking lot. I took my water and backpack and began the trek up through the banisters of neatly painted brown wood. As I began the climb, the most distinctive feature was the countless strips of cloth tied to the skinny branches of the scrubby pine trees: red, blue, green, yellow, and black. Many were filled, I knew, with tobacco to bless the land, the seeker's journey, and their ancestors.

In the initial zigzag ascension, I walked alone among the sandy, rock-strewn dirt holding the stubborn, crooked trees in place. Flat rocks became larger the higher I went, growing into boulders farther up the trail. Empty of other travelers, I wondered if this majestic site of sanctuary and importance had been forgotten.

Then I rounded a hairpin turn and was overtaken by a young, energetic woman wearing elephant ear–sized earphones. What wasn't usual was that she was carrying a group of prayer ties the size of soccer balls. She stopped to greet me with a wide grin and proceeded up the hill, at least twice as fast as I was, wearing black spandex stretch pants and a chartreuse sports bra. A bit stunned, I wondered if I had missed a more modern version of the quest that let you bring your electronics.

A local family with children passed me as I turned another curve revealing an expanse of muted green fields. I thought of Crazy Horse looking at some version of this view, carrying the responsibility he had taken on: a lifelong stand as a warrior to preserve his lands for his tribe. Now his people were fighting against the proposed building of a gun range on these very lands, which would remove the peace that had surrounded this site for generations. Some things haven't changed.

The path continued to wind its way up. The scrubby woods were deeper, the rocks bigger, the incline sharper, my water bottle emptier, and my energy waning. I could almost see the top. This side of the butte was practically vertical. Who knows when the treacherous switchbacks had been tamed into paths for the curious and devoted? The sparse trees were dwarfed by lonely hamlets of craggy rocks. A couple passed me going down. Only ten more minutes, they said.

I leaned into the slanted path. A modest wooden staircase appeared. I ascended onto a wide platform, a kind of boardwalk porch, that looked out on a 360-degree landscape of verdant yellowish green. The panoramic vista captured the flatness of the Dakotas with a sense of expansive majesty as I stood tall on the legendary promontory.

I had completed a ritual of my own design, and the months of anguish were in the past. I had done it without injury or forcing myself, using my own resources. I said a prayer of gratitude to the Creator for letting me have the life I had. Then I uttered another one to release what was past and scattered a bag of tobacco to make room for a new and stronger vision that expressed my core strength. I recounted my luck and gave thanks for all those who had helped me get there, including Crazy Horse and the many Sams in my life, who had held me up when I couldn't help myself. I burst into giggles and took photos until a boisterous group of ten arrived and destroyed the solitude.

I descended feeling as if I had gained a set of wings and lost twenty pounds of self-centered concern and angst. I hiked down jubilantly as I passed increasing numbers of families encouraging their children to keep going. Totally content, I crawled into my trusty metal critter, heaved a sigh, and headed home.

Chapter 17

Most endings aren't clean, like the snap of the tent pole in Badlands National Park. Even after my intentional ceremony at Bear Butte, persistent challenges continued to plague me.

In early 2017, I had a pivotal dream. I was the only passenger in the back seat of a black sedan on a crowded, fast-paced highway. I wore an oxygen mask with two tight strips of blue adhesive pinching my head. The driver was a short, dark-haired man sitting slumped down behind the wheel. He looked bored enough to nod off, oblivious to any risk.

We were driving onto a suspension bridge with girders as tall as skyscrapers. Four lanes merged into two. A red pickup truck approached rapidly from behind on our left, perilously weaving back and forth over the dotted white line, narrowly missing other cars. Leaning forward in the back seat, my stiff body was acutely aware of the truck and its reckless path. Although I could not see them, I was seized by a panicky concern for the truck's anonymous passengers. I desperately wanted to say to the driver, *Look to the left! That truck is about to pull into our lane and kill them!* It did not occur to me to worry about myself.

I had a choice: Should I remove my oxygen mask and risk suffocation to protect them? Or should I sit paralyzed, every cell in my body silently screaming for the salvation of people I couldn't even see? Which fate was worse?

Awake after the dream, I lay with my eyes open in my queen-size bed, its generous frame scrunched against the wall of my rented eight-hundred-foot apartment on the upper story of a duplex. My tiny bedroom had glass doors to a roof porch bordered by a set of majestic poplar trees. I crawled out of bed and walked barefoot onto the porch to look at the dusty pink sun rising over the trees, the dream gyrating in my head.

As I sat down at the small porch table, I could feel my heart rate increase, and I began to feel faint and tired. Checking my pulse, I found that it had rocketed to 140 beats a minute, marking the onset of an episode of atrial fibrillation. I went back inside and rummaged for the propranolol in my purse. I quickly downed two of the tiny pink pills and lay down on top of the blue-and-green comforter, its calming shapes reminding me of a New Mexico canyon at sunset. I prayed for my heart to slow down as my body vibrated, blood coursing throughout my entire system at an unwholesome speed. I practiced breathing slowly and turned over to my right side, feeling a slight sense of relief as the medicine took effect. As my heart slowed, the stark images of the dream faded.

I walked into the other bedroom, which served as an office, guest room, and home for general miscellany. It was stuffed with four IKEA cabinets, a daybed for guests, boxes of tchotchkes, including an engraved incense bowl my brother had brought back from Nigeria, and more than a dozen plastic bins full of photo albums. On the front of the cabinets, sheets of heavy art paper held lists of current projects written in blue, yellow, and orange markers. Most had red circles surrounded by the word URGENT along with a star and exclamation point. A piece of bright red paper was taped to one bin listing eighteen current projects with a title in caps: ANNUAL PRIORITIES. I vacillated between being incredibly proud of my lists and mortified by their haphazard size and scope.

Holding a cup of tea, I surveyed the room in my nightie that had holes under the arms. In deference to my heart, I chose to take that day off.

One of my rich trove of projects was volunteering at a kindergarten class with twenty-five students once a week. The girls covered their heads with hijabs. Their tiny figures were covered by robes in a myriad of colors from their heads down to their sneakers, including iridescent oranges, dusty blues, leafy greens, and deep purples. Their faces and hands were the only visible skin. The boys wore ordinary pants and shirts.

Most days, I worked with the kids around a miniature kidney-bean-shaped table. The young white teacher, a new college graduate, passed out worksheets containing pictures of objects with a line next to them. The assignment was to write a capital *A* next to the picture of an apple, a *B* next to ball, and then color the pictures with an array of crayons. Eager to serve, I put aside my feelings that my master's degree rendered me over-qualified for the task.

My assignment included witnessing a plethora of youthful conflicts that occurred as soon as the teacher walked to the other side of the room. One day, Ahmad, the slightest of the boys, leaned over and grabbed the coveted red crayon out of Ali's hand, his sleeve rising up and exposing a skinny wrist. Fawzia, the tallest and heaviest built of the children at the table, came from behind, tackling Ahmad. Her ample stomach pressed against his back, while her right arm squeezed his head against the table, as the left one pinned his arms together. She then adroitly grabbed the crayon, leaving Ahmad gasping for air. Sporting a triumphant grin, she clutched the prize in both hands and hastily performed an impromptu victory lap to a distant corner of the room.

The four remaining children rose in unified opposition, some with tiny hands on their hips. Others pointed their index fingers accusingly in the direction of the miscreant as they raised their eyebrows in righteous indignation.

"Hey, Miss Katherine. Look what she did!"

Pantomiming the fight, Ahmad said, "She pulled it away!" and folded his arms in a huff.

"Yeah! And I had it first!" Ali said, setting his mouth into a pouty line.

Although I was three feet taller and outweighed them by dozens of pounds, I was no match for their emotional intensity at being unjustly divested of the preferred crayon.

Meanwhile, Fawzia was sitting on the floor with her back to us drawing a picture with the contested object. She bore an expression of sly entitle-ment and thoughtful focus. Sitting peacefully in the corner, her previous act of pugilism seemed like a hallucination.

"Listen to me!" I said, to my four remaining charges, amazing myself by being louder than they were. It was enough to get the attention of the young teacher. Dressed in casual khaki pants with her sandy hair pinned on top of her head, she quietly approached the group and told them to sit down, producing some brand-new crayons as a bonus. She walked unhurriedly over to Fawzia in her self-created isolation and spoke some inaudible words into her ear. The teacher then confiscated the crayon and escorted her into the hallway for a substantial time-out. Her body and expression were as serene as if she were coming out of a massage.

My days at the school had a rhythm of highly charged action and almost reflective learning time. Lined up for recess, a covey of young boys, their bodies bursting with a need for movement, pushed one another to the floor. They became a spaghetti-like nest of intertwined arms and legs, heads struggling to stay aloft as each boy shouted for the other one to move. Another day, a celebrity read a story on the oversized video screen about a Black child winning a prize for writing a story in the sixties. Later in the year, a music teacher from the local mosque taught a song in her native Somali as the children sat with respectful attention.

On a special annual library sale day, Amah took my hand. She looked up at me, her face glowing inside her powder blue hijab.

"You know, Miss Katherine, my mom is so nice."

"Oh why?" I asked.

"She gave me a whole dollar to buy a book!"

"That's wonderful, Amah. What will you buy?"

"I like the one with the girl in the shiny skirt on the cover. I hope it's still there." She had a smile as big as the sky.

It began to dawn on me that helping a child learn the alphabet might not be my primary role. Was my job really offering encouragement and holding a tiny hand? Or letting a kid know that she was still accepted even if she stole a crayon or pinned a classmate to the floor? If so, we were equals. My heart ached for the same things the kids wanted: to be quietly recognized for who I was, to be touched and feel connected, no matter how unsure and inadequate I felt.

Maybe that was the point of all of my running. My frantic pace to accomplish an unwieldy number of projects was my unsuccessful attempt to forget my now absent marriage. I hid my disappointment in the guise of a frantically loyal volunteer, scurrying like a squirrel gathering acorns for the winter so I would be too busy to notice what I was missing.

I had another thought as I sat on my couch with Charlie and Lissa in my lap one evening after a day with my young charges. Perhaps I ran to reach a space of satisfaction and gratitude, a place where I didn't need to run at all. In some ways that had happened in the school. When I showed up calmly for the kids, they were able to show up for themselves in a light of happy brilliance. When they were shining, their reflected light gave me the inspiration and energy to show up for myself.

My contentment merged with exhaustion as my feline friends yawned. I joined them in my own version of an evening stretch of pleasure, and rewarded myself with a long, hot congratulatory bath.

Chapter 18

The years from 2013 to 2017 were marked by accelerated change. During that time, I lost my marriage, sold the family dream home I designed, moved out of the neighborhood I had lived in for seventeen years, said farewell to my college-bound daughter, advanced my career, and retired. It was time for stability and well deserved happiness, I thought. In the fall of 2016, I was unexpectedly pulled into the needs of a loved one.

"If Costco doesn't have it, you didn't need it."

This had been my stepmother's signature phrase as our clan gathered at my parents' house for holidays and special occasions. Rae Beth supplied only prepackaged products from the holy grail of retailers, which she had methodically stockpiled before we arrived.

"Do you need anything from the store?" we asked.

"No," she replied, "I have everything," even after grandkids had pilfered macadamia nuts from the pantry or created a suspicious hole in the Christmas yule cake.

My sisters and I first met her decades earlier when she became engaged to my dad. She was attractive and tall with straight black hair and well-proportioned features, wearing an eye-catching lime-green jacket and a black pencil skirt. On that first meeting, the look on her face was both anxious and welcoming, eager to take on the role of mama to my two sisters and me.

She had played the role of the caregiving matriarch long before my father's death nine years earlier. Following a stroke, she nursed him without complaint as he lost his ability to care for himself in the most basic ways. As a former elementary school principal, she was familiar with being in charge. Now, in 2016, she was managing the sale of the family home and her move to a senior facility with executive efficiency. She meticulously followed every business transaction as well as the activities of the seven grandkids.

I went to her home in Texas to assist in her move, although she never asked for any kind of support. When I mentioned my desire to help her move, she said hesitatingly, "Well, you know I have a company coming to pack."

As the boxes filled up in her living room, she had difficulty sitting still. The kindhearted women packed up her treasured belongings, ranging from a thickly lacquered black goblet she'd gotten during her missionary years in Japan to the double wedding ring table runner full of countless Christmas memories. We urged her to relax and watch.

"I feel like I'm doing nothing," she said, but she was smiling and deeply pleased, so used to being the workhorse after eighty-two years.

On the first night in her new senior living apartment, we sat on the familiar flowered couch among the half-unpacked boxes, emptying a bottle of wine. It was the most intimate we had ever been. Although I hadn't called regularly and shared with her details of my life, I had come to admire her unflinching dedication and commitment to my dad. She would never dream of saying no to any of us if we needed anything. She was an unconscious, unacknowledged rock in my life.

Concerned about her security but not wanting to pry, I asked in what I hoped was an offhand way, "So, how do you feel about the money part?" muffling my words in a glass of not so tasty merlot.

"Oh, I'm fine," she said, almost breezily, with as close to a drunken slur as I had heard in my fifty-four years of knowing her. She proceeded to share her financial details, which showed a level of canniness, savvy, and prosperity. I realized how little I knew her and how much I had underestimated and ignored her quiet intelligence and acumen.

Then she leaned over anxiously and asked about my nearly final divorce. "Are you going to have enough money?"

"Yes, I think so," I said, forcing optimism, though I was still uncertain. I was deeply touched by her concern.

I didn't visit that Christmas, which I came to regret. Shortly thereafter, she was making more trips to the hospital. I refused to heed the signs: the end was near. A heart valve transplant was scheduled for Valentine's Day 2017. I'd planned to go down and then decided not to. I chose not to hear the disappointment in her voice when I told her I wasn't coming.

Two days before her operation, my brother, Phil, called.

"She's unresponsive," he said. I got on the phone to the airlines and arrived in Texas that night.

In an effort to thwart the worst, they moved the surgery up to the next day, February 13. She lay in the hospital bed with her eyes closed, her body moving quirkily and restlessly a bit now and then, her eyelids fluttering but not open. It was easy to pretend she was just asleep.

Prior to the surgery, I walked around the bed touching her and praying; I had a strange sense of peace about what was going to happen. I summoned up the entirety of my ancestral faith in the hope that the hospital could fix her as they wheeled her into the operating room. My sisters and brother arrived, and we sat vigil together. According to the doctors, the procedure was a success, and we had a celebratory dinner giddily drinking mojitos that night, toasting her recovery. All we had to do was wait until she woke up.

But she never did. My brother, his wife, and the two oldest grandchildren were present when the nurses unhooked her from the beeping equipment that had kept her alive for two weeks. I was told that they saw a feathered angel carry her away.

My siblings and I had the dubious responsibility of cleaning out the apartment. As family members claimed pieces of her desirable jewelry collection, I found a letter to her from my dad. In his large illegible preacher's handwriting it said simply, "You love all the children equally."

I was deeply touched that she had kept this simple remembrance, especially because she was not a person who showed feelings or sentimentality. She had lived that resolve of equal affection for her three stepchildren and her much younger biological son. My father's acknowledgment of her quiet, unflinching support was far more precious to me than her diamond tennis bracelet or emerald ring.

We passed the front desk as we headed out of the retirement home she had moved into only four months before. Her smiling face was featured in their newsletter as a model resident, touting her success and authority as a principal. A neighbor said simply, "She was a queen."

I was familiar with death: I had lost my biological mom, my dad, my dear friend June, my father-in-law, and now my stepmother. I grieved for her the most deeply, hoping she was the last of a string of endings for a long time.

When I returned home, I went to a church service and remained in the pew after the ushers finished collecting the hymnals. In the empty sanctuary, I felt the crumbling of another wall that had kept me safe. All I wanted was someone to sit with me in silence the way my husband used to do when I was sad, silently holding my hand, providing a depth of comfort that came from a decades-long relationship where he had known me at my best and my worst. I yearned for a presence that said: *I know who you are. I know what you need. I know you are weeping. And I am here. Sit, lean on me, and don't be afraid.*

The only thing next to me was a box of tissues dimly visible in the cloudy February light. I continued to sit in solitude, acutely sensing the absence of what I had unthinkingly counted on, and my hungry desire for a human to recognize and hold me. This time, my grief was clean, deep, and palpable enough for me to squarely witness the hole in myself without running or getting distracted. Stepping into an unfamiliar pattern, I let the rawness pass and become part of me.

Chapter 19

One day in the summer of 2018, I had lunch with my friend Myra at a cafe overlooking the Mississippi River's limestone cliffs. The upper banks were topped by broad-leaved cottonwood and maple trees, boldly declaring the bounty of the season just two weeks after the summer solstice. The blue sky had a depth of color resembling a lapis set in a silver ring. The air held the early summer sweetness of wild bergamot and lilacs. We could see the scullers passing by in their long narrow skiffs one hundred feet below, the coxswain beating out the rhythm. They moved with the sleekness and unity of a millipede, passing under the bridge and making rapid headway as the instructor shouted commands through a megaphone in a nearby motorboat. At seventy-eight degrees with no humidity it seemed like anything was possible.

Every patio table was occupied with friends, couples, and families holding spirited conversations fueled by the stunning summer evening and verdant landscape. In the table next to us, a bearded man waved his drumstick as his gray-haired companion nodded, pushing his glasses back up his nose.

The server walked hurriedly by in a black apron, stopping briefly to deliver two local beers to our table along with artichoke dip and French bread.

"Let's toast," I said, as I held up my golden brew.

"Yes, to wild sex, happy kids, and more nights like this!" she said.

Laughing, we clinked glasses. As the alcohol began to go to my head on my empty stomach, I looked down at my hands and noticed for the second time that day that the joints were pink and swollen and my fingers were larger than normal.

"What's up with this?" I said, as I showed her my hand. "Do you think it's the booze?" I said laughing.

"Maybe you're allergic to something or it's just a seasonal change. Looks harmless, though," she said, as she took another sip.

"Let's say we're allergic to the beer, and they won't charge us!"

"Yes!" she said.

The Nordic evening mellowed while the sun gracefully descended, a disk of luminous orange. I continued to down another beverage, content while I finished the chicken kabobs and wiped my hands.

The next morning the swelling was worse and I felt feverish and lethargic. The sick feeling destroyed the joy I would have felt in looking out from my rooftop porch at the row of trees in their vibrant summer clothes. I got up to feed the cats and felt so dizzy I sat down. I stayed in my pajamas, ate breakfast, and then fell back down into my bed and resigned myself to a slow day.

The next day I felt worse. I stood in the bathroom and prepared to take a bath thinking the warm water would help. I glanced in the mirror at my left side when I saw a suspicious patch of pink. I lifted my breast and saw a bright red circle of flesh the size of a dinner plate.

I wasn't just a little allergic or tired. I had Lyme disease.

There was something good about knowing what it was. My discomfort wasn't in my head. I immediately made a doctor's appointment. It was the Fourth of July.

The fifty-something woman doctor entered the exam room with a businesslike stride, a stethoscope around her neck under her blondish hair with hints of gray. She listened to my self-diagnosis of Lyme disease and looked at the bull's-eye.

Her only words were "Oh wow! Classic!" before she wrote the usual prescription for three weeks of doxycycline. She did not question my opinion or do any tests.

I collapsed on the flowered tapestry sofa at home as my fever rose. My chest felt like it had been crushed by a boulder. Lissa and Charlie looked accusingly up at me, their tiny comma-like mouths demanding food with high-pitched meows. I was able to open the cans but fell and hit the cabinet when I attempted to pour the meaty chunks into their bowls. The fall left a purplish bruise on my knee.

I crawled into bed, and my thoughts became dim and fragmented. My bladder was filling, turning it into a painful, oppressive island in my belly.

As I attempted to make it to the bathroom, I had to fully concentrate to make my feet move forward along the cold, tiled floor.

I was scared. This is what people talked about with Lyme, I thought: a foggy brain and near paralysis that left them feeling unable to do the most basic things.

The notion of taking action floated dully in my head. I had asked friends to help when I moved heavy furniture, or packed and unpacked for my multiple moves. That was permissible—an able-bodied person requesting aid for a significant life change. People didn't expect you to lift heavy dressers and sort through years of accumulated cookware and heirloom jewelry on your own.

But this time my body had stopped responding to my bidding. Worse yet, my mind—my most dependable agent and guide—was following a dark, unfamiliar pathway that was both obscure and sinister.

Now clothes were on the floor, and the bathroom was developing an odor. The pile of bowls and coffee cups was brimming over the stainless-steel sink onto the stove.

My twisted mind began barking orders. It seemed to have transformed into a menacing samurai preparing for battle. I could picture a being in a horn-studded helmet with ornate strips of leather and metal on his chest, arms, and shins. He wore oversized, tailored boots capable of stomping on the enemy. This alien being began to speak in a deep, resonant voice.

Don't ask anyone to come. They would see the mess. What would you ask them to do anyway? Just clean it up! No one should see your mess!

And then: *What would they think of you? You wouldn't ask someone else to do* your *work, would you? You can't ask for help with a body that doesn't do your bidding!* I could feel him lean over with his hands on his hips, bent on intimidating me into agreeing with him. It was as if the warrior had a list of specific criteria for what was allowed, the samurai's code of shoulds.

My mind continued to skate in wobbly circles, unable to discern a plan for my unprecedented physical weakness and increasing fear of the bellicose being inside me.

Nonfunctional bodies are old people in nursing homes. It's okay for them to get help, the warrior declared. *They're done for and have earned the rest.* He folded his arms. *That's not you!*

I remembered helping my dad to the toilet in his final years. I held his arm as he trundled forward, hunched over in his blue terry cloth robe with his thinning gray hair on top. The once impressively powerful six-foot-two man was fragile and slow-moving. He shuffled in his worn brown leather slippers, the backs bent over where he had carelessly put them on. I helped him remove his loose sweatpants near the toilet as he looked directly at me.

"This is okay," he said, with resignation that hid his embarrassment. Ever the pastor, he said with righteous pride, "You're a married woman."

I couldn't imagine such an indignity for myself.

The samurai faded into the background as another voice emerged from inside me. *What's happening isn't me. This can't be me. This must all be punishment for not having a partner or the kind of friends I feel comfortable asking. Who am I if I don't have such a person to help me?*

I dimly heard the phone ring through the cacophony of misdirected voices.

"How are you?" Myra asked.

"I've got Lyme," I gasped.

"Oh, no! Do you want me to come over?"

"Yes, please," I answered without a thought. With that, my demented and confused musings vanished.

Myra came over dressed in a delicate yellow shirt with the top two buttons open. She had on gold earrings with a strip of silver. Her blonde hair was short, her bangs sweeping over her forehead. She looked like she was ready for a photo shoot.

I headed directly back to bed after I let her in, unable to stand. She hesitated in the bedroom doorway, staring at me as I lay supine, appearing timid and frightened at seeing me. I lay sweating in my purple-and-green cat pajamas, flushed with fever along with oversized, swollen hands and greasy unwashed hair. I could feel her unspoken upper midwestern mantra: I don't want to intrude.

She was as clueless as I was about how to help someone in a state of sudden, unexpected disability. The person now lying helplessly in the bed bore only a vague physical resemblance to the competent person she knew.

"What should I do?" she finally asked.

"You can feed the cats." With difficulty, I half rose and showed her where the food was.

"Maybe you could tidy up the sink. And help me to the bathroom?"

Awkwardly, she held out her arm. I leaned on it to travel the short distance to the toilet. She then withdrew, showing a combination of relief and embarrassment. I had temporarily become like my dad, but twenty-five years earlier than he had.

Gratefully, that phase of Lyme only lasted a few days. I rapidly put those nightmarish days behind me and assumed a life where I was once again thoroughly in charge.

.+. .+. .+.

I continued to work with another therapist to make sense of my emerging journey. A main benefit of this particular provider was meeting in her home office, which had a yard with a tantalizing, well-cared-for garden. Even in the middle of winter, her office looked out on inviting spaces with round tables, intimate latticed enclosures, grandmother elm trees, and artful brick work. In the warmer months, I was blessed to see lively bouquets of multicolored roses and lavender flowers hanging gently down a series of trellises over ornate iron chairs. In addition, there was always the enticing smell of blueberry muffins or a cherry crumble in the oven.

The counselor sat across from me, her short auburn hair hanging easily down her face and touching her turtleneck and small gold earrings. She had a way of welcoming me into her home with a smile, bubbling over with excitement at a new coffee cake recipe while receiving every comment I made as if I were an infant uttering my first word. I knew I could tell her anything.

When we were seated in the comfortable wing chairs, she began. "Tell me what you want to talk about."

"As you know, I've recently been diagnosed with Lyme disease. My specific issue is that I'd like to volunteer again at the school I worked in last year with five-year-olds, but it was exhausting then. Now with the limitations of the illness I'm not sure I'll be able to manage it. But I really want to do it!" I said earnestly.

"So tell me what it is you liked about it," she said.

"I think I just liked having children in my life." As soon as it came out of my mouth, I remembered what it felt like to pull the boys apart in the recess line and the conspiratorial look on Fawzia's face as she stole the red crayon. I remembered the treasured moment when Amah held my hand as well as what it felt like to come home too tired to take dinner out of the refrigerator.

"How did that work when you were there before?"

"Well, you know," I squirmed. "I did like helping them with their schoolwork . . . most days. There were some sweet moments with the kids one-on-one . . . but five-year-olds have a lot of energy."

She smiled and laughed. "Yes, they do! Tell me, what do you want out of the experience?"

I remembered attending the kindergarten graduation with the children dressed in bright red graduation robes complete with undersized mortarboards. The girls preened their shiny garments with their hands as they stood smiling single file in the hallway, anxiously watching for their parents. There were no incidents of children cutting in line or picking on one another, only quiet giggly conversations beaming with childish pride.

In the classroom party following the ceremony, the children and their parents received bags of candy and a farewell card. I didn't realize how much I longed to have a child press his or her small body against me, smile up at me and shout, "Miss Katherine! I'm graduating. Look at me!"

But the only child who went out of his way to thank me with genuine appreciation was Mohammad, the most difficult and angry child in the class. I had administered multiple disciplinary procedures to him. Otherwise I was invisible as children focused on their departing playmates and their grownups' approval. Parents anxiously asked the teacher how their kids could not fall behind over the summer and looked at me with a silent, distant suspicion.

I told the therapist, "I want them to know that someone cares about them, and I want a connection with them too."

She paused. "Where do you get your connections now? What's missing for you in your life now, Katherine?"

"You know my daughter is in her last year of college, and I don't have any family around here. I was hoping that the kindergarteners could be a substitute for her. But it's not the same."

"No, it's not," she said soberly.

"My daughter has been away for three years, and I miss her. Just . . . miss her." My voice started to break.

She smiled in the kindest way. "So what you are saying is that you want some deeper closeness, but you are in a precarious position health-wise and you doubt you have the energy to do this. I also hear you saying it isn't really providing what you wanted either."

The reality of her words stung.

"But I really want to do it," I said earnestly.

She smiled. "I know. I know. Just breathe and sit with me for a minute."

We sat together as her words rolled over me like a series of slow-moving waves. She had mirrored back the hole in my life while pointing out that working at the school was the wrong place, the wrong time, and the wrong solution for both my body and my heart. Even so, I felt a stubborn urgency about signing up again.

"I know you're right, but I still really want to do it," I said again, as I bid a sad farewell, softened by a generous hug.

According to Bessel van der Kolk in *The Body Keeps the Score*, our bodies store experiences that then predict the appearance and quality of what we call health or illness. I had collected responsibilities like refrigerator magnets, including tutoring the children and playing a lead role in multiple nonprofits. They were unquestionably noble causes. Unfortunately, the only consistent theme was a persistent exhaustion, which had now blossomed into a painful disease. The only cause I couldn't chair was my own.

My relentless pattern of running from myself had caught up with me. I now had to give up something that I deeply cared about. I would think of this insight bitterly as I continued to suffer massive attacks of fatigue and search for a peaceful connection to myself.

I resolved to stop being the consummate helper obligated to find a shelter for every homeless dog or two-legged being. I found myself recalling Holden Caulfield's sorrowful words from *The Catcher in the Rye*: "You couldn't rub out even half the 'Fuck you' signs in the world." But I could, I mused, wipe away the ones I had unwittingly written.

Chapter 20

Even in the worst times of my marriage, I could count on my partner to hold me with tenderness, his fingers stroking my back, my cheek next to his heartbeat. On the day we both knew the marriage was over, we instinctively held each other with gentleness all night, knowing it would never be possible again.

I thrived on touch, putting my head in his lap while reading a book. He willingly rubbed my feet and back, teasing out the cranky bumps and restoring a delicious blood flow that allowed me to feel a sense of vibrancy about my life. I didn't think I could face a life without such tactile connection. If the marriage was my skin, I was now a burn victim, my life-giving sheath singed, unable to protect or nourish me. I went into a shock-like withdrawal, missing the soft fingers I had come to rely on, feeling like a baby with failure-to-thrive syndrome.

Several people told me to find a good massage therapist. I smiled and nodded, but they were missing the point. There was no way the best masseuse could replicate the touch of the man who had stood by me through so much, stroked my hair when I had a tough day, and even agreed to another child when he was in his fifties. The vessel of my body bloomed on affectionate, loving contact, not contractual services.

In her essay "High Tide in Tucson," Barbara Kingsolver writes about a part of Arizona that used to be underwater but is now bone-dry and arid due to environmental changes. Some creatures, she claims, still have biological functions in tune with the ancient rhythms of that place, as if the long-absent salty liquid was still flowing in obedience to the commands of the moon.

Like those ancient creatures, my body yearned for its old cadence, my husband breathing next to me, snoring quietly sometimes, yet comforting always. When he was absent, I slept fitfully. On his return, I fell asleep in a few minutes with my arm on his side. The consistent tempo of his life force sustained me as well as him.

My body still sometimes feels like a puppy that has been unwillingly yanked from its canine mother, abandoned to a human home. Part of me resembles those dependent creatures, pushing my nose against the blanket, trying to get as close as possible to a missing human heart. Sensitive new owners often put a ticking clock inside a blanket to comfort these young whelps.

Some years after my marriage ended, I started sleeping between two pillows. I used them to hold myself together in a way the marriage did, my daughter did, and my notion of family did. When I embrace a cushion in front of me and put one at my back, a calmness rises within me. They are physical reminders that I need both boundaries and softness. Unlike some containers, you can throw them away, donate them to a shelter, or buy lavender-colored pillowcases on sale when you get tired of them. I care only that they provide a fluffy sponginess that seems to welcome me to myself, as my breath slows and I ease into sleep.

I pull closer to the pillows in my queen-size bed with the woven coffee-colored headboard, scrunching into the puffy cushions that have become my surrogate family. I imagine myself surrounded by everyone I love in the past, present, and future. In a moment I fall asleep, having cajoled my flesh and psyche into a space of nourishing darkness and the delicious reward of rest.

Chapter 21

Homer's epic poem, *The Odyssey*, weaves the tale of Ulysses' archetypal quest to return to his beloved home in Ithaca after a momentous victory in the Trojan War. His adventures include seven years on the island of Calypso, where basically nothing happens as he idly gazes at the sea. He finally reaches his home after wandering for twenty years. Since he is physically, emotionally, and spiritually changed, his suspicious wife demands proof of his identity; she finally recognizes him and then joyfully welcomes him.

Likewise, the Mayan creation story, *Popol Vuh*, recounts how the gods accomplished their divine purpose of crafting the human form. Their first effort resulted in a totally perfect being, void of even the most minor blemishes or flaws. As they examine their shining prototype with pride, the gods realize it simply won't do. The peoples who would inhabit the earth would fail miserably, embarrassing themselves at the most inopportune times. They would—by necessity—learn to tolerate all manner of frustration, injury, and heartache. A perfect body couldn't endure a life full of continuous struggles. So they destroyed their first attempt and remade the human figure with appropriate warts and beloved defects. *Popol Vuh* teaches us that it is more deeply human to err and recreate ourselves than hit the mark the first time, which leaves no further reason to continue the quest.

During Ulysses' solitary tenure on the lonely island of Calypso, he was disoriented, frustrated, and puzzled as to why he couldn't move forward at the pace he so desperately wanted. I felt his yearning for his native Ithaca as well as the *Popol Vuh*'s curse of imperfection as I went to endless open houses looking in vain for a new place to lay my head. Knowing that the failure to achieve one's ambition is an archetypal dilemma didn't help.

Exasperated, I asked a teacher why a house—a nurturing dwelling—wasn't appearing after moving twice in two years.

She said, "You won't find a home until you find one within yourself."

Her words were not welcome. Like Ulysses' time in Calypso, I had stepped into a period when it seemed that my actions yielded no fruit. In my mind, I was doing everything possible to advance and grow, and I did not appreciate the intimation that I wasn't succeeding on my spiritual path. I considered myself the most dedicated of supplicants.

In 2018 I finally found a house that deepened my comfort with myself. It had taken three years and three moves. Strangely enough, the house had been for sale the first time I looked two years before, but I hadn't had enough money. On the market again exactly when I needed it, I snapped it up.

By the time I moved in, my new home had been vacant for two months after being rented for two years. The unkempt foliage was so thick you couldn't even see the three enticing cherry trees. In a drizzly rain, I pulled out dandelions, creeping speedwell, and groundsel as my fingernails turned brown and grainy. In two short days, a generous covering of mulch replaced the weeds, and the hostas formed an inviting garden under the shade of a French lilac tree.

As I looked at the fresh seedlings and newly tilled ground, I was stunned. What had been an abandoned fragment of renegade weeds was now a patch of serenity and care. My life could do that too. My uneven path of recovery could become peaceful and fruitful at any moment, just as the garden would soon boast scarlet geraniums and plump cherries. I was capable of developing and emitting a lively and vital energy—if I gave it room to grow.

I once heard a song about a wise man who walked straight to the tree, while the fool wandered around endlessly, unable to locate his destination. I wish I could say that I was the wise one, but I can only say I am equally the fool, mirroring the journeys that have been told in myths and legends by the most ancient of bards. The only thing I know for sure in my spiral journey is that the divine has my best interests at heart, and that the great mother does not think I am a total schmuck. For me, one of the most important teachings is: when it gets hard, go deeper. I have tried to listen to my higher self even when cloaked in anger, grief, despair, and unfathomable discomfort.

Even though my new home seemed perfect, a year after I moved, I found myself already weary of it and wondering what life held for me next. My restlessness told me I was changing, but this time I wasn't afraid. I was able to see that the uncomfortable feeling was merely indicating that life's river was taking another turn. I no longer viewed my anxiety as a threat, nor was I invested in keeping things the same. This new path had the potential for adventure and surprise. Yes, it would probably also contain disappointment; but I was beginning to trust my burgeoning strength to handle the unpredictable and see that a true home is a place of flexibility and change, not a rigid container as I had fought so valiantly to preserve during my marriage. There was no need to leave my house because there was a trace of unease. The stuff of living is to continue to peel the layers away and look deeper, find a practice that works, have faith, and not be shy about asking for resources to help.

Four years later, the garden was flourishing, full of phlox, stella d'oro daylilies, columbines, butterfly weed, sedums, tomatoes, and kale. It was still the best place to lie down with a blanket and doze in the sun contentedly, with a ginger cat's paws spread out on my chest.

Chapter 22

No matter what choices I made, images from my former married life continued to resonate within me. Some remembrances were keen sources of solace while others elicited heartache and a yearning for bygone times.

Visiting friends one summer weekend, with delight I discovered a sauna on the porch. Stepping into it, I was hit with a vibrant memory of the smell of burning wood, the moist heat of steam rising from rocks, and the lazy family togetherness we enjoyed in this Nordic shelter.

My former husband was of full blood Finnish descent. In both of our houses, he painstakingly designed and constructed a sauna in the basement. He chose the cedar boards with care, so we wouldn't be poked in the bottom by a jutting splinter, and nailed the structure into a cozy haven. For the second one, he was aided by our two-year-old daughter, who amazed us by accurately identifying a socket wrench from a group of tools sitting on the floor. The completed structure became a place to quietly witness sweat pouring out of our overheated bodies. When we weren't using it as a sauna, it served as a place for meditation and prayer, comfort seeping from the cedar logs as we left behind our active, demanding lives.

John instructed me in the proper etiquette and language of his native convention. First of all, you had to pronounce it correctly, giving it three syllables: sa-u-na, not "sawna" as most locals said it. I had to learn to use a wooden bucket, the unique accessory to this Scandinavian tradition. Its high rounded paddle stuck up several inches for use as a handle. As the sauna reached a scorching temperature, I was instructed to use a giant wooden spoon to carefully dribble the water on the rocks. As the steam rose, the liquid made a sizzling noise like meat hitting a hibachi, increasing the already suffocating heat.

While I came to treasure the sauna in our home in town, the one at our cabin in the north woods seduced me into the custom forever. It was the only heat source for the small lakeside dwelling, which had been built in 1945 by a fellow Finn. The old stove was ancient, its metal walls thinner than a tin can, yet capable of heating the chamber to two hundred degrees with a searing fire. You stayed in until you couldn't bear it any longer. As the sweat began to roll down your body, you could gaze out the window at the lake, pines swaying past the panes; or, you could peek out at the white trunks of the birch trees, resembling sentries in the cluster of greenery. Real aficionados often whipped their companions with birch tree leaves, a kind of affectionate S and M bonding game.

When you had absorbed all the heat you could stand, you took a dip in the frigid lake. After completing this process three times, you sit and have a beer and watch the sunset, savoring stillness and a cleansed body and soul. The two long benches were lovingly wiped down after each session. Finally, it's time to play cribbage, the hot fires of purification having ignited your competitive spirit.

The cabin sauna became a sacred refuge for our family. Its memory is a source of nourishing solitude. I smile as I remember my daughter's childish request to paint my nails with pretend polish at age three, the unhurried conversations about the water level in the lake this year, and the softness of my body when the heat had frightened the impurities out of every pore.

In those moments of remembrance, the sauna is not a thing, but a living being in my memory, like a captive DNA strand of the best of times. The sauna bucket, the wood, and the scorching air are physical expressions of the enduring nature of blessing in my life, a gift symbolizing the love and mystery that has made me who I am today.

Its memory is a vibrant, comforting resource I am grateful for. Other items, especially the photos of Jenna as a teenager, bring forth a yearning wistfulness.

My daughter chose to attend college on the West Coast, half a continent away from me. My time with her grew shorter and shorter with each passing year, as she began to fashion a career and develop relationships away from home. Sometime after she moved out, I found a stack of pictures of her with an impish grin when she was in high school. She was flanked by two friends, one raven headed and another with brownish locks, their hands sitting jauntily on their hips, with smiles boasting expressions of infinite youth, strength, and daring.

Unlike the sauna bucket, which brings up only affection and softness, the photos cut to the heart of what I most deeply miss. I remembered Jenna and her friends cooking pasta and throwing it jubilantly at the wall. They laughed hysterically as they took videos of the cats jumping to retrieve the sticky noodles. Another time, they shot molasses-soaked cookie dough up in the air, creating a sticky brown mosaic on the kitchen ceiling. I responded to requests for items such as walnut oil or crimson embroidery thread. A flurry of activity followed in the frenzied creation of an exotic salad or an unconventional sewing project. The only predictable element was superlative energy and snorting guffaws that made me plug my ears with their volume.

As I looked at the photos, a forgotten voice whispered: *I used to live with people who loved me and laughed with me. Young people with piercing voices came to my house unannounced and gave me hugs. I asked about their moms and siblings as they produced kitschy skirts to wear or a tasty main dish with ingredients available only in western Borneo.*

And the sober pronouncement: *I used to not be alone.*

The realization was more stunning than sad. I had actually forgotten the quality of youthful dynamism that was an effortless, assumed part of my life for so many years. It amazed me that the fun of connection had left my brain's portfolio, replaced by a life that is quieter and savors the preciousness of raucous gatherings and less common hugs. How can we fail to recall something so fundamental and life giving? It is because, as Hermann Hesse says in *Journey to the East*, humans are destined to forget.

It is, I admit, especially wrenching when a dozen smiling families at a cocktail party brag about their children who live in town and have become engineers and successful brokers. I invent reasons to hate this group, but in sober moments I realize that my resentment cloaks my sorrow—an older woman, my only child living half a continent away, with no surprise young people or lover for whom I am the first priority.

David Hawkins, in his book *Letting Go*, talks about allowing oneself to feel the depth of sadness to the bone, fully experiencing one's own vulnerability, welcoming any emotions that arise, no matter how unwanted. In accepting them, one finds the way home, releasing the depth of grief.

His approach helped me navigate the depth of my own self-imposed suffering. I had become an expert at nursing my sorrow, as I simultaneously ran from it, breathlessly pursuing any distraction. I realized that I was ignoring life's inescapable lesson: let go, or you are forever shackled. Acknowledging that my daughter was really gone put me in touch with my rawest emotions, allowing me to unapologetically shed a new and familiar set of tears.

For years I easily convinced myself of my signature brand of agony, buffing it with devotion until it morphed into an armor of impermeable defiance. When I stood on that dais of self-pity, in my confident prideful resolve that life had wronged me, I was left with a frigid isolation as bleak as a sunless winter day. My stubbornness gave me permission to reinforce the sorry and boring saga of my entitlement to victimhood, as constant as the waves on a sandy beach but without their comfort. The repetitive commitment to my version of the story failed to shield me from my visceral sense of estrangement. Hawkins's invitation to total surrender acted as a poultice, drawing out what no longer served.

I deeply miss those days of family time together—from the sweaty evenings in the sauna to the buoyancy of a giggling bunch of girls. With my growing willingness to let go, I have done my best to count my innumerable blessings. I am loved, and I know it. Just because the people who care about me aren't sitting in my living room, their affection is no less real. I have overwhelmed my journal with words about treasured friends, the love I still feel for my ex, a daughter who adores me even if she isn't here to hug me, and a growing sense of humor and regard for the person I am becoming.

Chapter 23

I was privileged to continue my visits to the cabin after our marriage ended. I avoided going for years after our separation, fearing it would evoke painful memories of what had been a place of cherished joy. On my first trip back, I found I was delightfully mistaken. I enjoyed myself fully, with my only dark memories being the lingering shadow of separation I felt when I was there with him. His primary activity was finding weeds to whack or eliminating spiders from the boathouse as I lost myself in a book or swam in the chilly water, feeling a dull but palpable sense of distance between us. On my own, slow days at the cabin were a joyful surprise. My solitary visits became occasions to claim a new space for the individual I was becoming, not someone's wife or mother.

I was, therefore, unconcerned when in the summer of 2018 all of my companions reneged on joining me for a cabin outing. Going solo was fine with me. I was longing for the smoothness of the water and the heat of a wood sauna. I wanted to sit in the outhouse next to the blue spruce, watch the hummingbirds, and stare at the whimsical wind stirring up gentle swells across the lake.

I drove up the unpaved, pebble-strewn road with its patchwork holes filled with muddy water, passing the signpost with the names of every family on the road. Many of them had been there since the forties, and some had been John's babysitters. I gingerly drove down the hill to park in the tall grass at the end of the point and was overwhelmed with an unexpected sense of loss.

Twenty-five years ago to the day, I had gotten married at a church as an ecstatic forty-two-year-old first-time bride. Family and friends had come with jubilation and well-hidden relief. A limousine had taken us to a friend's house for a fairy-tale lakeside reception. A harpist strummed sweet ballads from the gazebo that overlooked the water under sheltering oaks, accompanied by my sister on the violin with a bow in her long hair matching her long pink dress. The tables were festooned with white table-cloths under an ornate beige tent, the posts draped with pink ribbons and calla lilies. The gourmet picnic lunch included sun-dried tomato pesto, penne pasta with chicken, braised zucchini, and a hazelnut and carrot wedding cake. The day concluded with a circle dance ending at dusk in the August twilight, all seventy-five of us together in the fading light with our clasped hands raised together. About thirty guests stayed on the spacious screen porch as we opened gifts of placemats, china, and silverware to raucous applause.

Arriving at the cabin so many years later, each moment of that magical day began to play in my mind, along with the familiar wrenching guilt of having pulled my family apart by making the most difficult decision of my life.

The shattered joy of our wedding day leapt out of my body as I opened the padlock to the back door. I walked down the half-broken cement steps painted white to keep us from stumbling in the dark when we wandered outside to peer at the stars. I stepped onto the dock that had been built by a happy family crew on a festive occasion when Jenna was eighteen months old. On the wall was a picture of my stepsons triumphantly haul-ing the old dock away by boat. That weekend had concluded comically as the whole family fled the cabin, running from an irate group of yellow jackets displaced by our construction. I shielded Jenna with a rain jacket to keep her from being stung.

I stepped into the sauna, my healing haven for hours on a chilly, rainy, northern Minnesota day. I had become accustomed to stretching out on the cedar benches, my body savoring the remaining heat from the night before. It was also a sweet reminder of my dear father-in-law, Art, who loved to have the sauna on low, maintaining a small, measured fire with the skill of his eighty plus years. I knew he was there when a puffy gray cloud floated out of the chimney, a sharp contrast to the thick, dark plumes created by our fierce attempts to raise the temperature as quickly as possible.

I thought of a time before our marriage, when John and I tuck-pointed the chimney with concrete. With an upbeat smile, he assured me that the task would take two hours. Eight hours later, we were still mixing low-quality cement to repair the crumbling structure. I recalled our first summer as a married couple when we, at John's behest, hiked down a snowmobile trail, trudging for hours with boggy, muddy water up to our knees. We watched the mosquitoes bounce off the screens on a glorious evening without electricity, with nothing to do except focus on the tiniest creatures inhabiting mother earth. As we merged into child-rearing, we followed the fireflies with other families, dashes of light moving like a flock of tiny luminous birds. On other trips, friends played board games after the young ones fell dramatically into the water like a Marx brothers' film, comically mimicking a Shakespearian death.

That evening, I looked across the lake and saw the reflection of light on a fishing line as an angler cast his rod in a perfect arc. The neighbor's seaplane taxied across the half mile of lake and began its ascent. I wistfully looked up to catch a sky the color of a late summer melon. The joy of the life we had and the regret that it was gone returned like water rushing through a broken dam, an unwelcome companion during what was supposed to be a few solitary, relaxing days.

As the late darkness fell in that northern place, I thought of an IMAX movie I had seen years before about the launching of the Hubble telescope. The photos showed swaths of pillowy, vaporous brightness light years across. Their magical presence would challenge any notion that there is not a profound, otherworldly force in the universe.

The narrator told star voyager stories about the mysterious pictures. Along with multiple shots of inexplicable black holes, there were shadowy glints of space dust looking to hook up with other particles, a kind of celestial pin the tail on the donkey. Over millions of light years, the particles clotted into the miraculous spots of light that we call stars. The narrator described this immense galactic birthplace as the star nursery.

A star nursery! I was mesmerized as I gazed at a place where baby stars grew up until they were ready to shine by themselves. In this cosmic playgroup, they would inch forward with an unsteady step on one of their little stubby five-point star legs. Slowly, they graduated to crawling across to another buddy star that was standing in its crib. The special nebula dust helped their precious arms grow pointy and strong. After several more millennia, it could get out of its crib and confidently ascend, taking its place as a star itself, supplying light and direction for mortal beings for eternity.

Watching the film, I had been transfixed by those images, and began to imagine my own relationship to these nascent stars. I found myself asserting, in a dreamlike state, that my true identity and destiny was to be the nanny of the star nursery. I was the matriarch responsible for creating brightness in the universe, for making sure that the stars would shine and the force of luminosity would continue, sparking inspiration, love, poetry, music, and songs in the past, present, and future. This was not a declaration of hubris or pride, but a deep knowing that my destiny was to provide a cosmic level of support to these magical starry beings above.

That night at the cabin I could not have been farther from declaring myself the heavenly guardian I had claimed to be so confidently years earlier. On that summer evening, my conviction about my sacred role on this planet was all but gone. Instead, I sat on the metal-framed futon between knotty pine walls with a visceral, cloying loneliness.

I felt a despair reminiscent of my first Halloween in 2013 after John moved out. At that tender time when the division between the worlds of the living and the dead is thinnest, the ghost of my mother appeared in the house, her image as solid as the oak dining room table. An anger arose I had never felt toward her, starting from my toes and climbing into my heart.

I had called my friend Helen and asked her to come over. An extraordinary friend, psychic, and counselor who had predicted my divorce, Helen had been a constant source of empathetic support. She came right away and agreed to be my mother's stand-in as I talked to her.

Me:	*Screw your illness! You left me alone with my wacko grandma and raging, volatile dad!*
Mom/Helen:	*Yes, I did.*
Me:	*I was a kid. It wasn't fair.*
Mom/Helen:	*I did what I could.*
Me [screaming]:	*How dare you!*

I railed at Mom/Helen for what I didn't get to say. Helen held me steady as a child, oblivious to my waterfall of tears.

For decades I had held a memory of my fragile, pathetic, sick mom with pity and sadness and parroted my dad's line about the reason for the divorce.

"She couldn't take care of you. That's why she had to leave," he would say morosely, as he pushed his eyeglasses up his nose. It was many years later that I heard the word "schizophrenia" applied to her.

The only actual victim of my story had been me. My rightful fury at this early loss should have been sent powerfully outward, yet the thought never occurred to me. Holding it inside me created a volcano of self-blame nothing could touch, manifesting in hostility, depression, separation, and a food addiction. That night with Helen I was able to do what I had never been capable of: voice the ire of that painful, unfair abandonment that had left me with an overwhelming burden of my own guilt in a situation in which I was blameless. The anger that had festered within me for so long had finally found a way out.

As I spoke, I realized that experiencing the bitter loss of my marriage had uncanny similarities to my mother's departure, creating a crushing, double angst. Two devastatingly sad events were linked in my psyche. It didn't matter that I had chosen the ending of one of those relationships. All I knew was that I had hidden an honest and justifiable rage behind an arc of sadness. Until I could vomit out my wrath, it remained stuffed inside of me, keeping me a desperate and hopeless child. In claiming the rage, I was granting myself the power of adulthood and its accompanying agency: the same authority I was taking in ending my marriage and giving up the too familiar feeling of powerlessness.

After Helen left, I had a dream. My husband and I were in full evening dress, he in a tuxedo and me in a gown with elbow-length gloves. We were radiantly dancing on an elegant ballroom floor, happier than we had ever been in our married life. It was as if my confession had freed the furor in my body and my dissatisfaction with him, allowing both of us to glide gracefully into a new life.

An extraordinary friend helped me cauterize and heal a hidden, festering wound that had stunted my growth, not only in my marriage, but in my actions as a capable adult. That unexpected Halloween night became a time to get to the core of my own darkness and glimpse a freedom that had eluded me.

⚜ ⚜ ⚜

In my blithe arrogance on that night with Helen, I thought my despair would not return. Here I was at the cabin, many years later, in a familiar place of despondency.

At 3:00 a.m. I walked outside to pee and looked up at the stars, proud and full without the dimming effects of city lights. Perhaps six thousand or more of them formed a canopy over the lake a half mile in either direction. They just hung there: Orion, Cassiopeia, and the Pleiades, barely discernible as the dots of their compadres littered the skies in an order as precise and ancient as a perfectly prepared game of heavenly cricket.

The stars were suspended in the sky with no help from the fragile humans below. No matter what I did or how I felt, they would be winking countless generations after I am gone. Yet, somehow, I was sure they knew my agony and guilt at ending my marriage to save my soul in a way no human ever could. Their job was just to shine, and mine was to gaze and be comforted.

By the time I went back to bed, I understood a whole new truth about the star nursery. The stars themselves were the nannies, whole bunches of them! They carefully walked around on their shiny star legs and picked up humans who had forgotten who they were and their most sacred and intimate dreams. The stars held the vulnerable humans tenderly in glowing stardust blankets. This time one of the humans was me.

I was nestled in a comforter as soft as the fur of a fleecy llama. Six-pointed star nannies were twinkling to console me as if I were a treasured grandchild in their starry arms. They cuddled me as closely and tenderly as you would any infant, touching my hair, smoothing the blanket as they softly whispered how beautiful I was, how brave, courageous, and persistent.

I had thought of myself as the nanny of the nursery, but they were in fact the nanny of me. Each nanny took this charge seriously, connecting me to the forces of the great spirit and reminding me that I was a beloved, treasured, capable human destined to live a life of joy and ease.

Humbled by the loving message from above, I sat on the dock and stared as my heart glowed with this newfound knowledge. In a state of gratitude and awe, I walked back inside as a shooting star streaked across the sky. Unsurprised, I smiled at this very unsubtle wink from the divine, reminding me to take heart as I looked ahead.

Chapter 24

By June 2019, I had spent months silently berating health care practitioners who treated me as if I had the sensibilities of a melon. After spending thousands of dollars, I experienced only brief periods of relief as the debilitating symptoms of fatigue returned. At a session for people with health challenges, the group leader asserted that one of the biggest traps of healing is expecting that it is your doctor's responsibility.

I blanched. A part of me very much wanted someone else to be accountable for banishing my Lyme disease. I wanted them to chase away the wily borrelia bacteria that had set up housekeeping in every cell of my body.

I could defend myself with the knowledge that I had done my part. I had said prayers with the urgency of a novice nun while eliminating sugar, dairy, and grains and taking handfuls of supplements. Given my dedication, not to mention the amount of money I had spent, the notion that a practitioner wasn't responsible startled me like a sudden gust of wind. Couldn't I dump a little of this on someone else?

But denial is a resilient critter. When I saw a healer, she took one glance at me and said, "You are full of grief," and strummed and sang over me for hours as I lay under a soft woolen blanket. The next morning, I sobbed uncontrollably, forcing me to consider that she might have touched a place I couldn't reach on my own. In my mind's eye, unbidden pictures appeared of my generous former neighbor who meticulously sewed a Halloween costume for my daughter as our family went off to my father's funeral. I remembered giggling, blindfolded girls putting a tail on a donkey at my daughter's seven-year-old birthday party. Recalling happy memories of a life I no longer had revealed that it was not physical disease but another layer of grief that held me back.

Fortune smiled on me. Friends invited me along on a trip to Ireland—an adventure to the friendly land of fiery, undaunted Celts, a crooning Bono, and the lyrical poet Yeats. Of course I would go, even though I was still experiencing one or two good days a week and then a day or so in bed. During the long winter months, my body begged to cancel the trip as the fatigue and body aches zapped my energy. I quit every nonmandatory activity for two months to give myself a chance to make the trip.

An additional challenge was traveling with my daughter, a national-level athlete, who would accompany me as my college graduation gift to her. While other kids might come home from school, pounce on the couch, and demand hot chocolate, Jenna took great interest in the Theraband my physical therapist had given me. She Googled band workouts and spent the next thirty minutes splayed out on the floor strengthening her pecs for another Ultimate Frisbee tournament.

Ultimate players run about seven miles per game. On a tournament weekend, they routinely play three to four games in a day. This had been her life since she was fourteen. At twenty-two, she was recognized nationally for her skills, endurance, and commitment to the sport. She had even missed her graduation ceremony to support her college team, leading them to a number five spot in the nation. I swallowed hard as I thought about her expectations of me to keep up with her. I dreaded feeling like a wounded sheep struggling to keep pace with the flock. Nevertheless, she was excited, and I wasn't going to let this increasingly rare opportunity pass us by.

My daughter's choices for sightseeing included the Guinness Brewery—the number one tourist site in Ireland—and the Dublin jail. I picked a historical walking tour, which I came to bitterly regret.

Settling into our comfortable quarters, our innkeeper shared with downcast eyes that, yes, he was divorced and remarried, but only because he liked the taste of wedding cake. On a local radio show, a singer waxed on about his Scots-Irish heritage, which surfaced when he wanted a bit of grog but was never keen to pay for it. It was soon clear that the Irish were not only chatty but had a humorous, long-winded storytelling talent that gave me the gift of frequent chuckles.

The historical tour I had chosen was scheduled for ninety minutes. The enthusiastic guide pontificated for well over two hours, telling us more than we ever wanted to know about Michael Collins, the vicious Vikings, the uncompromising Catholic Church, and Ireland's fierce, hard-won struggle for independence. At minute ninety-seven, I whispered to my daughter a desire to leave. Holding her phone like a reunited lover, she looked at me as if I had told her to wear jeans to her own wedding.

"I'm not leaving," she said, folding her arms, her rigid stance making her look far taller than her five-feet-four inches.

"Why not?" I asked.

She narrowed her eyes.

"You *chose* this. You have to stay." The edict was pronounced with a sinister glare.

She turned away with a look of contempt and triumph that explained why sportswriters had called her "relentless." This quality was now being applied to an obscure tourist ethic I had somehow missed. I found myself wondering if the energy I had put into raising her would have been better used by breeding ferrets and getting them to learn the Hallelujah Chorus. After she asserted her personal moral code for travel, she spent lunch glaring at me with an unapologetic smirk between sips of soup.

Our sightseeing complete, she prepared to take the bus to Limerick and join her organic farm volunteer group. I would unite with a group of women to tour sacred sites. Part of me couldn't wait for her to leave so I could take a break from walks that had the intensity of a Marine boot camp. I told her she could take a taxi to the station, at which point the multiple personalities of her fledgling adulthood opened a tiny crack. She looked at me like a five-year-old being sent off to kindergarten.

"Please come with me," she said, close to pleading.

I was silent. I knew she was going to be all right, and I desperately wanted to nap before I joined my group. I finally gave in, and she recovered her stance of belligerent superiority. Charging ahead, she frequently turned to me with a familiar simpering grin.

Time is as flexible for the Irish as a kindergartener's Play-Doh, and the bus was nowhere in sight at the stated departure time. I was ready to leave her there when she made an imploring request to stay with her until the bus arrived. Knowing the days when she would admit she needed me were few, I stayed. As the bus appeared, she climbed on, steady and poised, the emerging adult reappearing, confidently waving goodbye.

⁌ ⁌ ⁌

I joined my touring companions, eight older white women united in a desire to explore Ireland's mysteries. Our first site was Newgrange or Brú na Bóinne, its circular white walls stretching for almost an acre. Older than Stonehenge, the edifice rises out of a verdant meadow with an aura of strength, stability, and mystery. The milky-quartz exterior and rounded, grass-covered roof stand more than forty feet high. The welcoming kerb stone at the entrance contains a series of triskele figures, ancient Celtic triple spirals that represent earth, water, and sky.

The guide invited us inside with a caution to those who were claustrophobic. We entered the structure one by one, walking through a narrow stone hallway. The passage was no more than thirty feet long and well lit. It ended in a round enclosure about twenty feet across, where we gazed upward at a small-domed ceiling and a narrow slit in the front of the dome. Only at dawn on the winter solstice—and sometimes a few days on either side of that date—a streak of sunlight shines through the opening for seventeen minutes, making the chamber luminous. Some thirty thousand people apply to a lottery for the coveted fifty places to witness the darkness turn to the light on the longest night of the year.

I was transfixed at the simplicity, elegance, and purpose of this chamber. What was this fascination with year-long obscurity and the all too brief spark of its partner light? Perhaps the purpose of this building was to hold and honor the nurturing power of darkness—a force I had spent the last few years running from. Could it be that I had missed the point altogether? Was this lengthy dwelling in blackness actually the true touchstone of healing? Was this fleeting glimpse of light only a brief, necessary counterpoint to allow us to appreciate the eleven months of shadow? Was seventeen minutes a year of light long enough for a vibrant renewal, and they knew it? What knowledge did they have that we have lost?

I didn't want to leave. I could have turned off the lights and stayed there all night, snuggled up under the stony dome, like a newborn awaiting my own birth. Instead, I walked out, stood in the field, and looked silently at the circular edifice, astonished at its content and story. I sensed those who had gone before and created a place where people can still relish the power of darkness and its luminous companion—light—five thousand years later.

My encounter with this spark of radiance would have been enough, but a mere thirty minutes away is Teamhair, or Hill of Tara. The legend is that the anointed king touched an obelisk-shaped rock called Lia Fáil or Stone of Destiny. The mighty stone phallus shoots up from a megalithic mound, the precise spot where the anointed king received the transmission of divine power. The site invites reverence, surrounded by brick-shaped stones laid into the ground in the shape of a resplendent sun.

Fintan the Elder, a voice from Celtic lore, declared, "Ireland is a wheel, and Tara is its center." Indeed, this quiet place is an unmistakable landmark that can be seen for miles. Energy fields called ley lines surround the area, forming a powerful network of healing.

I lay down on the earth, feeling the magnetic force penetrate my tired, illness-ridden body, surrounded by Ireland's lakes and misty hills. It didn't matter that it had been hundreds of years since the royal ritual had occurred. Its vitality, both powerful and soothing, remained, and I didn't have to be a king to receive it.

⚜ ⚜ ⚜

Ireland is different from the rest of the British Isles as it was never conquered. The Roman armies retreated because it was too cold, too far, or they'd spent themselves raping and pillaging Great Britain. As I waited in line to purchase a heavy woolen sweater to thwart the June chill, I understood why it might not have been a target of domination.

Our tour sandwiched places of profound spiritual significance between sites of ridiculous, belly-laughing mirth. Outside of Cork, we visited the

Michelle and Barack Obama oasis: a gas station with a bronze statue of the couple waving enthusiastically in an unintentional resemblance to Mary Tyler Moore. The proud property of President Obama's eighth cousin, the inside of the gas station hosted life-size murals of the helicopter that brought the two distant kin together. Next to newspapers that boasted of the unique Irish Tidy Town Awards was a photo of Obama and his cousin waving to the crowd with their arms around one another, grinning like schoolchildren who had successfully sneaked out for the day.

Minutes away from the incongruous scene at the petrol station was a stone circle dating from 4600 BCE. The stones were oddly shaped, including squares and rectangles and flattened circles, some as tall as me. They were covered by a white shell-like fungus that made them appear ancient and strangely welcoming, as if they were decorated just for us. Rowan and willow trees stood as quiet sentries at the gates. I could almost hear the bards and priestesses singing ceremonial songs, their rituals palpable as the emerald grass inside the ring of stones. The kindly spirits seemed to amble silently about, protecting us as they had previous generations.

Our ultimate destination was the Hill of Uisneach, the geographical and spiritual center of Ireland, which we would reach on the summer solstice. We prepared for this climax by holding an ending ceremony at a nearby St. Brigid's Well. Each of us walked barefoot around the pool to a stony spring, cool waters seeping into a dark pond. As we stepped down into the water on the moss-covered steps, we were anointed with a loving hand, the watery blessing preparing us for the sunset on the longest day of the year.

I had expected crowds as we entered Uisneach for this celebrated change of cycle, but only a modest group walked up the hill. We passed the statue of the earth goddess Ériu —Éire in Gaelic—who represents sovereignty. Our guide was an older, wiry man in shorts, with disheveled gray hair, his voice as expressive and full as a deep-throated bell. His monologue ranged from high screeches to a somber throaty bass as he shared the land's mysteries, his entire body animated. I was humbled by this eccentric being and his love of stories. He had clearly jumped time to be with us.

"Ériu married the sun god Lugh," he said with excitement. "They discovered seasons here," he said proudly, noting how the sun god moved in its elusive way, causing the crops to thrive as well as the earth to sleep. He laughed when he forgot what he was saying, as if life were a cosmic joke we enjoyed together.

Like Newgrange, these pre-Celtic people knew how to use and treasure the darkness. Hundreds of underground caves still remained under where we stood. They had been used to hide livestock when they saw warring tribes in the distance, as well as to store grain and hold rituals. I had no trouble imagining small groups of frightened humans in homespun clothing urgently making their way to a secret passage under the dirt, fleeing from attacking forces. Equally, I could imagine a covey of priestesses preparing an offering in honor of Ériu and Lugh. As the guide talked, almost all of the Americans fidgeted and looked at their watches, finding his story hopelessly boring, while the Irish sat enraptured.

We continued to walk past torches set up for the solstice ceremony site. Perched on this promontory, at least ten counties were visible from the highest point, with patches of verdant farmland in the distance, along with rolling chartreuse hills. At the moment of sunset, we all looked at the panoramic view, a feeling of reverence uniting us. It was broken by the introduction of a guitarist from . . . New York! The crowd could not have been more thrilled or appreciative, clapping and cheering with gusto, their Irish sense of wonder and hospitality effortlessly flowing out.

The next day we returned to see the major attraction and sacred site: Aill na Mireann, the Stone of Divisions, that marks the exact center of the country. It is commonly called the Cat Stone: it bears a rough similarity to a cat squatting over a mouse. It is an awkward, unwieldy thing, weighing many tons and rising over twenty feet in the air with sizable outcroppings and space underneath large enough for a human to nestle into. Legends say this is the burial place of Ériu, a sanctuary of the feminine.

We approached the gravesite with a deep reverence, our guide insisting that the women go first in silence. We touched it as if it were a delicate treasure, running our hands over it, some of us lying down underneath. The rock and our group of women became a sculpture of basalt and flesh braided together, as if our female bodies had found their home in this five-thousand-year-old rocky icon that had nurtured so many for so long.

I experienced an almost forgotten connection with an ancient spirit celebrating both the feminine archetype and the precious notion of sovereignty. Perhaps this is what my quest had been about. I fiercely wanted to embody an interior strength as mighty as this ancient rock. What an extraordinary privilege to meet the qualities I wanted to manifest in such a proud, iconic form. We reluctantly finished our pilgrimage, walking silently down the hill in sober observance and gratitude of this tangible expression of the divine, placed there, it seemed, to bring us to a deeper discovery of who we were.

❖ ❖ ❖

I could barely walk three thousand steps a day when I began the trip. By the end of the journey, I was doing eighteen thousand. Somehow, I was channeling an energy I didn't recognize. The trip to Ireland healed me in a way that no physician or medical protocol could have. We little understand the invisible forces that continue to play with us, like a river that changes course after a flood, fashioning a path that we do not recognize yet continues to deliver growth, delight, and miracles.

Chapter 25

Back from Ireland in July 2019, Jenna and I spent a few days rebalancing our biological clocks as we slept during the day and watched romantic movies at night while munching Wheat Thins and Colby cheese. We dedicated ourselves to picking sour cherries off the three trees in our yard, which were bent heavy with fruit and on the verge of turning dark and sour.

On those sweltering summer days, we wore aprons stained with crimson juice and stood in the kitchen carefully pitting each fruit individually with a mechanism resembling a hole punch. Prairie women had done the same exhausting job with this crude tool a hundred years earlier. Our wrists aching, we boiled the fruit with mounds of sugar. Jenna grasped the hot soupy mixture with wooden pliers and gloved hands, pouring it into the Mason jars I held, as steam burned our faces. To our great satisfaction, friends raved about our hard-earned confiture and declared it worthy of a state fair ribbon.

Our reverie together was short-lived. The final tearing of the cloth happened quickly. She had planned to return to Seattle for a short time, then come back home to Minnesota for a few weeks in late summer to take a part-time job. That plan evaporated when she interviewed for a job in Washington state on Thursday and received a job offer on Friday. She accepted it on Monday, bought a car in Minnesota on Tuesday, and came home for twenty-four hours to finish the paperwork and drive it away. I had counted on the brief visit home to soften the blow of her decision to live out west. Instead, in the space of one week, she established her independence and destroyed forever my illusion of control.

Another container was being disrupted. This time, it was my role as mother. My baby had become a full-fledged adult. Even though she had lived half a continent away for four years, she remained under my protection and sponsorship while she was a student. When I cosigned a lease, helped her find a doctor, and accomplished countless smaller tasks, I was an important and needed matriarch.

It didn't matter that she would be in my life forever. I felt only that a familiar and reassuring form—a child in college who came home with regularity—was gone. A job I had loved like no other was coming to an end. The people mourning this loss—the empty nest syndrome—were usually fifteen years younger than I was, still enmeshed in their careers. Now, with my working life and marriage over, and with an unwelcome focus on my health, it felt more like the empty soul syndrome.

One morning I awoke at 3:33 a.m. I hadn't slept decently for over a week. In my foggy state, I knew that my insomnia wasn't accidental, but about my daughter taking flight. That summer she had lived with me for the better part of six weeks, more time than we'd spent together in four years. I had gotten used to her energy, humor, and buoyancy. We had hiked across the United Kingdom, seen castles and oceans, and learned to laugh at our inevitable clashes. We'd watched the US women's soccer team win the global title, with her experienced and snappy commentary.

"Where's the defense?" she had said, with hands on her hips seconds before the commentator asked the same question.

I had withheld my opinions about where she would live post-graduation, adopting a debonair neutrality, knowing she would purposely do the opposite if she knew what I preferred. Intellectually, I was okay with her being out west, as I sensed she would be happier there. I had sagely told others that where she lived after college was in the hands of God. Now that she was gone, I felt hijacked by the clutches of Satan.

Having experienced weeks of total happiness and satisfaction, I arrogantly thought I had mastered this unpredictable life voyage and conquered my demons. My heart, however, knew my rational explanation was a lie. No matter that her new job was only an eleven-month assignment. That didn't stop her decision from feeling like someone had ripped out my wisdom teeth without Novocain.

Everything you have ever had will be taken from you. This is a lesson of life that I was tired of learning.

I chose to take life's rock-solid assurance that this unbearable feeling of loss would abate. But it was hard to believe, as I felt its intensity grab my heart with ferocity. I thought of all the losses over the last years. My marriage was central, but I also endured a growing number of deaths: my friend June with her Alzheimer's, my father and stepmother, my father-in-law, my friend Virginia, my extraordinary friend and psychic Helen, and my biological mom. They were all gone. Their stinging absence flared up like a pile of blazing autumn leaves, the universe barreling into a space that doesn't know time, making me feel as if the losses were all happening at once—again.

There is a song I have sung to hospice patients:

There are angels going round
There are angels going round
There are angels going round

The lyrics help me remember to call in what I need at this moment. I thought of Helen saying to me years before, "There are a thousand angels in this room protecting you." In my mind's eye, I saw the gentle creatures with their feathery wings bumping into each other, arguing, smoking cigarettes, and crowding the room to comfort me. I felt the bounty of love in the universe as the angels moved forward to help me.

What can we do for her now?

Mable, get out your harp!

Seth, try the guitar.

Ezekiel, put your arms around her!

At that moment, I was an eight-year-old who had lost her mum. And now I had lost my daughter through geographical distance. She still walks the earth, but my role and relationship with her had entered an uncharted, unwanted, and undefinable phase. I sighed in disappointment, recognizing that the whole episode was more about me and my mom than about Jenna.

The feeling changed from pinpricks in my abdomen to a softer place, as if the pain was going to sleep—and I imagined myself lying in front of the TV with Lissa and Charlie curled up on me as the angels bent over me with quiet soothing hums.

I remembered that I was the nanny of the star nursery—and they were the nanny of me. Stars were still being born, and I would recover with greater strength, elevated to be *their* nanny, the one who nurtures them.

I climbed into one of those luminous cribs and pulled a blanket up to my chin, with the aid of the other star nannies. They were all bent over my crib of light, stroking my head, picking me up, and passing me around with concerned and loving looks on their faces as they comforted this seemingly inconsolable infant.

Each one had a different way of bouncing me—some held me to their heart; some looked at me directly and spoke star baby talk. Others made faces that looked a bit like a monkey with indigestion, reminding me of a nurse reviving a fainting newborn.

Shhhhhh it's okay—I know . . .

I fell asleep with a sense of cosmic well-being. The boundless grace of the universe had eased my pain, and I felt a sense of love and safety with the cooing in my ear. The nannies knew their only mission was to express timeless love and compassion that is the unshakable birthright of each being on earth—animal, vegetable, mineral, and human.

As the nannies discharged their job with tenderness, the force of grief receded, falling away to a sense of well-being and knowledge that I would always have this love sustaining me no matter what happened.

With a breath of thanks, I closed my eyes and entered gratefully into the field of dreams. I would face this grief even though I wanted to run, run, run, run so nothing could catch me. Somehow the stars slowed me down, and I understood in a way I never had before that I didn't have to run anymore.

Chapter 26

I have always had a strong belief in the spirit world. Its magic, strength, and vibrancy continued to surprise me as my journey continued, and was starkly apparent when I hit a wall.

I had thought I would have fully recovered from my divorce in two years. Years later, I agreed with the horrifying testimony of several divorced friends. They didn't feel like themselves, they confessed, until seven years had passed.

One day I was meditating while feeling a kind of "Why me? What the hell?" despair. Two figures appeared before me: a man with a long reddish beard and a woman wearing a long white robe with a look of serenity on her face.

"You are almost there," the man said. "Use what you have. Don't be afraid to focus on what you really care about. Trust that your solace is coming. Do not despair."

The arrival of these figures had me take heart.

The mechanism of time had become a curse. The scholar and researcher Jean Houston asserted that cancer is a disease of time. Cells misfire at the wrong microsecond, losing track of what and when to attack, unable to discern the difference between a nourishing or poisonous presence in the body. Like a malfunctioning white cell, I kept thinking that if I could just get to a certain calendar date, I would be guaranteed a sense of effortless well-being, kind of like having a lifelong supply of valium without side effects.

Yet I continued to feel like a half-baked cheesecake. The eggs, flour, and cream cheese were combined and smooth, the oven was the right temperature, the stove alarm had beeped completion, and yet I was still a jiggly undercooked mess. I had successfully executed numerous strategies to solidify my well-being, including working with multiple therapists, learning spiritual practices, spending time with friends, volunteering, and traveling to places known for renewal. Although these pastimes offered moments of joy, my center remained soupy and wobbly, with the consistency of a half-baked pudding.

My fervent desire was for happiness—unbridled, jubilant, unending. *Please God, give me a whiff of it. I won't be selfish! I just want a fleeting smell,* I would croon, as I stealthily plotted how I could greedily hold on for eternity.

I am humbled by Ezra Bayda's words in *Beyond Happiness*: "Each of us must examine how we get in our own way. . . . our sense of entitlement that life should go the way we expect it to go." I had worked hard to shift my focus, attempting to welcome any circumstance, no matter what life threw at me. As Bayda suggested, accessing stability, gratitude, acceptance, and love offered a stronger guarantee of serenity than I felt I was entitled to, a sense of cheerfulness just because I was on this side of the dirt.

On those days when I needed to return to the rock inside of me, I turned to my own ancestors. I lay down to sleep and saw the face of my beloved Aunt Geraldine.

"Look at little Kathy! You're the prettiest thing-g-g!" she would say. I remembered the day when I was six and trying to play Monopoly before I could read. I sorted out the first three letters and colors into groupings. She looked at my work and beamed, calling my dad.

"Mouzon! Look at what little Kathy is doing!" Her unconditional affirmation of my playful task warmed me like a freshly baked chocolate chip cookie. The memory provided a resource that filled me up and made me feel radiant and special.

An extraordinary healer, Belleruth Naparstek, talks of calling on "all the people we will love in the future." Likewise, in a Tonglen meditation practice, I have imagined all my loved ones from seven generations in the past and in the future forming a protective circle ten deep around me.

Naparstek's phrase makes me feel as if the oxygen around my body has doubled and a magical cloak of protection has descended upon me. I will no longer need to worry that I will be alone and deserted. People I have never met already love and treasure me. My end of the bargain is to trust that they are here to support me. Many nights I have fallen asleep with my hands on my heart and stomach, knowing that they are really my mom's hands when I was a child or those of Aunt Geraldine. I know this with the same confidence I have that my daughter will always love me.

I have also been profoundly changed by the teachings of an ancient Mayan tradition and their concept of allies. Learning this wisdom in the sandy hills of New Mexico gave me the courage to leave my marriage more than any other single thing.

In the eight-sided medicine wheel, each direction has a specific meaning and intention. An ally sits in each direction with a distinct name and purpose. Mine have introduced themselves to me, and I have a strong sense of their identities and how they can assist me. They are real beings to me and have appeared in some of the direst of times.

The first time I realized their power was during an exceptionally emotional period while on retreat in New Mexico. I became disoriented and hyperventilated, collapsing on the ground. I was panicked that I wouldn't be able to find my way back to the center and shrank fearfully against the rusty earth and tree trunks bent askew. Without delay, all eight allies showed up and walked me back to the retreat house, no more than five hundred feet away.

These cosmic friends wear unique colors and wardrobes. They are proud of their idiosyncrasies. Allied Forces Lead the Way stands in the east, encouraging creativity in a bright yellow jumpsuit complemented by a leather apron. Laxmi sits in a meditative pose in the southeast. An Indian woman from the subcontinent with long, raven hair in an orange sari has a bindi in the center of her forehead and wears an expression of utmost tranquility. The androgynous, playful Samantha has a wicked smile as she stands in the south. Their hair is helter-skelter in a lopsided bun, and they're dressed in a short, gathered skirt with yellow leggings and a bright red shirt. In the southwest, the magenta-clad Pathfinder looks toward the horizon, reminding me of my own legacy and gifts when I have forgotten who I am. Miriam in the west resembles a focused and benevolent mother. Her long purple dress and outstretched arms welcome me in the times when I need healing the most. Eagle's Wing, a lavender figure with wings for arms in the northwest, reminds me that each cycle will end, and another will begin soon. Blue-vested Arrow in the north advises me on the best actions that honor both the brain and the heart when I feel overwhelmed by heady thoughts and gut-wrenching emotions. Lastly, Orion in the northeast takes pride in changing their gender, skin color, and voice to remind me that life is not a fixed game.

My eight allies have an incredible sense of humor and teach me about living in the moment, as they take action with extraordinary, loving spontaneity. They regularly take me shopping, changing what they wear according to what my mood and being needs. If they are coming to liberate me from an act of lifeless obligation, they are likely to show up in a Batmobile, new outfits flashing on each one of them. Laxmi dons gaudy sunburst earrings. Allied Forces wears a luminous, sunlike suit with a metal vest and saddle shoes that would make Elton John swoon.

On those low days, when I am down at the river, they surround me and give me a group hug, each one with a giant pack of Kleenex to wipe my dribbling face. As I heard from the voice on the wind in those early days of this journey, the resources are always there. Now, they reach out like octopuses of compassion, holding me up as I climb the bank back to my house.

I no longer underestimate how much these unseen forces can help me. They aren't silly or unreal. I have needed every single one, and I am learning to accept the gifts they unfailingly offer.

Chapter 27

After yearning to return for years, I finally went back to New Mexico in September 2019. I reveled in the spacious purple sky, the vermilion earth, and the expansive valley with its muddy S-shaped river and rusty banks. This was the site where I encountered liberation from the beliefs that held me hostage and ultimately led me to leave my marriage. It is where I learned that healing can be synonymous with pain and where my shrouded courage began to wiggle her fingers, bend her toes, and test out a few tentative syllables that were truly her own.

I had driven up the dirt road many times before, the potholes just as perilous as they had been almost a decade ago, reminding me I was glad the car had a high carriage. No matter how snazzy the vehicle, the journey still resembled a badly designed amusement ride at a local fair.

I took a turn and started to ascend. I could see them up ahead: the obelisks that marked the property's entrance, resembling a celestial warrior work project accomplished thousands of years ago.

This land was a living, beloved friend, inhabited by silent boulders, red dirt, and ambling waters. I got out of the car and looked out over the ridge lined with piñon trees, scrubby little fellas tough enough to tolerate the fierceness of the heat, the onslaught of snow, and the minuscule amount of rain. I walked to the canyon's edge and stood on the flat gray rocks as I had so many times before.

The river was below, creeping along with the lethargy of a recently fed coral snake. The surrounding trees were still green in late September. With sunset's receding light, dark shadows crept down the hills, which resembled the lounging body of a voluptuous woman. The smoky purple clouds hovered like bird wings over the shadowy land. The entire scene felt like a teardrop of God, a gift of a passing bodhisattva, in compassion for these silly and overanxious sentient beings.

The ghosts of the past seeped through me as I hovered on the solid edge. I remembered the day I had a panic attack and unseen allies led me back to the house. The day I sat on the ground and felt the sadness of what seemed like every human flowing through me from the beginning of time as I deeply felt my mother's illness and departure. The afternoon I listed the limiting beliefs I held about my marriage and saw that it was my own ideas that were the most virulent. The people who had sat with me when I saw without illusion what I was hiding from. The raucous laughter as we performed a skit where I was a bawdy country western singer with a Texas twang. My extraordinary friend Lightning Feather, with whom I shared a bond beyond time and who died two years later, meeting death with equanimity and love. I saw my confrontation with my own demons and how peeling away the layers had allowed me to move forward.

The inflexibility I brought to this land years ago had robbed me of my own sovereignty. Now I no longer needed to look to others to give me my authority, direction, purpose, or well-being. I knew that any structure that appeared to be tight and secure—a job, a relationship, a belief, a place—could kidnap my spirit and serve as a platform to relinquish my ability to be in command of my own life. I felt as confident as a general and the goddess Athena combined, secure in my life path and hard-won knowledge. But most important, I had a deep feeling that I've got this, not just in ceremony but in life too.

I walked down the hill and saw a new teepee with a cement base that had been erected the day before. I entered and noticed tufts of juniper surrounding the firepit as well as a pot of dried roses in tobacco, ready to be offered for prayers. The teepee wasn't large and could hold only about twelve people. It was just my size.

I sat down and took a pinch of tobacco in gratitude for my journey. Every bit of it. I felt embraced and honored. I said a prayer, welcoming myself home.

Epilogue

According to my psychic friend Helen, cosmic forces are constantly work-ing behind the scenes to get everything precisely in place. Though one's life may appear completely static, the energy of change is moving at a steady clip, and the preferred outcome will reveal itself at exactly the right time.

If you had told me on that painful morning, eleven years ago, that I would still be single a decade hence, I would have considered myself the inhabitant of a loveless and painful life. Although I am not partnered, I am experiencing life as a whole, complete person with a satisfaction I could not have imagined before.

When I walked away from that teepee in New Mexico five years ago, I did so with a sense of modest triumph. I thought my healing was com-plete. I could check it off, and I could tackle my next adventure: Life 3.0.

Although I thought I didn't have a timeline for healing, I kept falling into the engineering mindset that parts of myself could be reconstructed or replaced, like the aging boiler in my century-old house. If I took the correct course of action, like going to another retreat, dedicating myself to daily meditation, or spending a fun game night with friends, I could escape a sinking feeling of despair. I had chosen to ignore reminders that maintaining my own well-being and emotional health could not be put on an Excel spreadsheet.

Today I know that healing has a rhythm as complex and enigmatic as a Beethoven symphony. Some days the drum will beat softly, on others the trumpets will nearly knock you over like a wave at the beach that catches you when your back is turned. The beat, timing, and instruments of healing may change, get louder or deeper, softer or more textured, but the song itself doesn't end.

We are always healing something. Each time we move forward into a new place, another wound opens that is ready to be transformed, and we cannot hurry it or choose its topic. If you find this notion a bit abstract, let me tell you a few things that have happened since that sweet moment in the teepee in 2019.

After attending twelve-step meetings intermittently since the eighties, I finally achieved abstinence from a chronic eating disorder. I did so with the help of a daily discipline, an insightful nutritionist, a loving community that holds me consistently accountable with compassion and connection, and the grace of God. For the first time, I am confident in my new eating patterns. I have permanently shed my clothes in sizes 14 and 16 along with my consumption of alcohol, sugar, white flour, and dairy products. Previously, I couldn't have imagined losing my dependable and nonjudgmental food friends, even though they kept me in a state of desperation, failure, and self-condemnation. I refused to see that this destructive addiction blocked any solid, authentic growth as well as intimacy with others.

I had told myself my disorder "wasn't that big of a problem." I was overweight, but by no means morbidly obese. My persistent overeating had damaged me for so long it felt like a part of me, not a separate, life-sucking behavior. I began each day on a diet, stuffed myself within two hours, and hated myself by the end of the day. Clad in unrelenting shame, I had no confidence in my ability to change. Abstinent from my food addiction, I became keenly aware of how my damaging habit contributed to the dysfunction and distance in my marriage and other relationships, to consistent denial, and to ongoing mood swings.

As my obsession with eating receded, I was able to see what was really missing. In the strange mystery of the COVID-19 lockdown, I found true self-intimacy, maybe for the first time. Relieved of my countless list of activities and an overabundance of food, I sat in front of the fireplace petting my cat Charlie with a sense of blissful satisfaction. I saw how many of my relationships and undertakings were empty and unworthy of my attention. Following the isolation of that unprecedented time, I have turned many long-term friendships into deeper, treasured companions and let go of others that no longer served either of us with a sense of relief, humor, and power. These actions have given me a heightened sense of agency that I truly relish.

I have also become acutely aware of the depth of my own despair and the patterns of thinking and isolation I used to cope with them. Due to the help of some extraordinary healers, I have faced the darkest pieces of myself and found tools to deal with my trauma and the deep-set depression that was the legacy of my childhood. I continue to learn and to search. The up and down journey of the last eleven years has evened out, and I now have a deep compassion and love for myself I couldn't have imagined earlier.

A wise teacher recently told me that the divorce—traumatic as it was—gave me the life I was supposed to have. Operating from a new place of stability, I can now agree with Helen. The great mystery has been rapturously pulling strings behind the scenes with a sly and mischievous grin. My new feeling of authentic renewal *has* happened at the right time.

Was there a turning point? It might have been when my dear cat Lissa, the ultimate alpha cat, was diagnosed with cancer. It never occurred to me I would lose one of my two cats while I was still single. Her diagnosis reminded me what both cats meant to me, and I began kissing and talking to them, treasuring them both after taking them for granted for years.

I let Lissa go on an April day one month into the lockdown. At the moment of her death, I felt her spirit soaring out of her body into the next realm with a feeling of joy and electricity. I cried for a few days, but the intense sadness passed.

Likewise, when Charlie met his end, I held his sweet body with his orange paws touching the earth as the vet administered the final shot. I was also able to grieve deeply but quickly pivoted into gratitude for his countless hugs as he sat on my lap while creating this manuscript.

The most wrenching surprise and most difficult teaching has been John's unexpected health crisis. He had remained a deep and dependable friend, helping me with knotty housing issues such as a mold infestation and a neighbor who wanted to run a truck through my backyard. He also offered patient and shrewd advice as we became better friends than lovers.

We thought he was the picture of health as he played pickleball three times a week for more than a decade. In November 2021, he had a triple heart bypass, which appeared to be successful. However, he refused aftercare and I noticed a gradual but significant decrease in his cognitive abilities. In August 2022 he was admitted to a hospital and transferred to transitional care for rehabilitation. By the end of September, he accepted that he could not return home and would have to take residence in an assisted living facility. After a slew of horrendous misdiagnoses and mismanagement in the health care system, it was finally revealed he had had a series of strokes, ultimately leaving him unable to walk and with limited speech.

These unexpected events sparked my past patterns of catastrophizing and doom. I walked in grief and panic as I attempted to direct and control the situation in a number of fruitless ways. Ultimately, I was able to see that the best thing I could offer was my presence. I visit him regularly, hold his hand, and show him videos of Finnish travelogues and live eagles so he has a fleeting sense of the outdoors. He has retained his sense of humor, laughing as he points to the similarity between his hair and the spiky points of his year-old great grandson. They look exactly alike.

The house in which I lovingly designed every tile and chose every paint color was torn down by the new owners. They also cut down the maple tree that had become my muse. The universe was soundly declaring: This phase of my life is over. Another chapter awaits with keen expectancy in the wings, which has included the return of my daughter to my community.

Grief continues to rearrange me. The illusion of stability is forever gone as I have walked gratefully with teachers of all kinds, including the sultry vibrations of my choir. For perhaps the first time, I am proudly claiming my strength with the sober knowledge that I was trained to succumb to weakness and had even enjoyed an identity marked by powerlessness. But here I am, my strength and confidence growing, launching a new career in spiritual work.

Maybe that's the point: just love it while it's here—your cat, your lover, the petunias in your window box, your kids, grandkids, and community. Just give it everything you've got, cry like hell when it's gone, and turn around and see with new eyes what's still there. Love never ends. Grief never ends. My job is to accept the circumstances with love knowing we are all imperfect.

If I have learned anything, it is that life is a neverending opportunity to discover strength.

Acknowledgments

Nothing happens without a group of people standing behind you, beside you, and in front of you. This book is no different.

This is actually the second book I have written. The first one was about the earliest segment of the rocky road, which was bumpier and hopelessly dramatic; it ended with the breakup of my marriage. It was a tome of documented dysfunction rather than courage. During the trip to Ireland, the visceral sensation of lying beneath the stone of the sacred feminine convinced me that people would be more nourished by a journey of developing strength than hearing every detail of a broken relationship.

I was blessed to have many voices who preached the twin gospels of self-confidence and hard work. The no-nonsense words of Hope Langner, Rick Tamlyn, Chuck Lioi, and Sabrina Roblin relentlessly confirmed that I had something of value to say. At the same time, they kindly and firmly made it clear that there would be no book without consistent hard work and striving to go deeper every time I wanted to run from the keyboard.

I am deeply grateful for the support of the writers' community in Minnesota and across the country. On the days when I could hear the radio station KFKD (K-Fucked in the words of Anne Lamott) very loudly, the voices of countless community members provided assurance and encouragement. Women of Words (WOW) Saint Paul and my writers group provided words of cheer through countless drafts. The Writers' Colony at Dairy Hollow in Eureka Springs, Arkansas, provided the space for my first draft. The ARC Retreat Community in Stanchfield, Minnesota, hosted me royally numerous times to help bring this project to completion.

Many generous, talented individuals read my manuscript with seriousness and made critical, essential suggestions. They include Sandra Eliason,

Louise Miner, Judith Brenner, Karen Mueller, Laurie Phillips, Teri Mc-Namara, Carter McNamara, Ann Mathews-Lingen, Kathleen Welcome, Royce Holladay, Suzanne Begin, the late Gloria VanDemmeltraadt, Meridian Johnson, and Ann Elliot.

I would like to particularly acknowledge Beth Wright of Wright for Writers LLC (wrightforwriters.com) for her long-term support, shepherding this manuscript from a concept to the printed page. Her steady presence and broad knowledge of the writing and production process was invaluable. Rachel Moulton also provided structure and insightful feedback.

If I have forgotten to mention your contribution to this project, I ask your forgiveness. I am profoundly grateful to each one of you, and I regret I didn't record the names of each person that supported me in some way. Any omission is my responsibility alone.

Finally, I want to thank my family and friends, including my ex-husband, who have stood by me during this project, asking how it was going with genuine concern and interest through its long birthing process. Special thanks to my daughter, for her ever insightful and salty comments. You are the best!

Healing Resources

My journey included many organizations, individuals, and modalities that helped me move forward into a more powerful, stronger identity. I am including a few of them knowing that each of us needs help at some point.

Regarding my eating disorder, I am deeply indebted to the individuals in Overeaters Anonymous (oa.org) with social thanks to the HOW program (oahowphonemeetings.com). They taught me that compassion and connection are the antidotes to an eating addiction. Their written literature and regular contact—often several times a day—provided invaluable support in allowing me to find freedom from this debilitating illness.

The Dynamic Neuro Retraining System (DNRS) (retrainingthebrain .com) provided an invaluable tool to reset my thinking patterns and substitute positive images for trauma-filled memories.

The principles of nonviolent communication helped me find a new way to interact with others, balancing self-responsibility and respect for boundaries. I especially appreciated the insights of Yvette Erasmus (yvetteerasmus.com) for her generous advice and counsel.

The Ehama Institute (ehama.org) and Dancehammers (www. dancehammers.com) provided teachings in ancient wisdom traditions that gave me courage, insight, and the will to action.

Buddhist teachings were also a great comfort. Common Ground Meditation Center (commongroundmeditation.org) and the Lotus Institute (thelotusinstitute.org) provided great solace and spiritual support.

Finally, I would like to acknowledge and recommend the work of the Institute of Spiritual Healing (instituteofspiritualhealing.com). Through the writings and chants of an ancient Sufi tradition, their work provides a deep connection to the divine.

The resources are always there. May you find the ones you need.

You may reach the author at rockyroad2137@gmail.com.